The Lincoln Authority

How to Lead with Authority
in Today's Organizations

Keith N. Miles

The Lincoln Authority

How to Lead with Authority
in Today's Organizations

Keith N. Miles

Streamlined Press

Toronto

thelincolnauthority.com

The Lincoln Authority by Keith N. Miles

Keith N. Miles is an author and management consultant who lives outside Toronto, Canada. He received his BA from Western University and his MBA from Wifrid Laurier University's School of Business & Economics. He is President of Streamlined Management Group Inc., a management consulting company specializing in leadership, organizational change management, and performance-orientated organizational culture change.

For special purchases: *http://thelincolnauthority.com/contact*

To contact him: *http://smgknowledge.com/contact*

Table of Contents

Dedication

This book is dedicated to Raymond J. Mulder, who demonstrated the exercise of firm and positive managerial authority. He inspired a career-long interest into what is truly the core responsibility of leadership.

Acknowledgements

The Lincoln Authority has been a team effort. I wish to thank the following talented and discerning people who contributed in a significant way to the development and formation of the book: David Armstrong, Laura Bunyard, Kenneth Edwards, Sandra Halloran, Deirdre Healey, Michelle Josette, Nancy Miles, Neil Miles, Liz Miles, Raymond Mulder, Amy Outland, Mark Rutledge, Brian Schofield, Lindsay Stark, Gordana Terkalas, Brian Tithecott, and Gordon Wehner. Cover Design by James, GoOnWrite.com

I would also like to extend my special thanks to Lewis E. Lehrman and the work of The Lincoln Institute and The Lehrman Institute. His dedicated efforts have created an outstanding series of educational websites about Lincoln, especially Abraham Lincoln's Classroom. These websites contain articles which describe specific aspects of Lincoln's life, for example: his character, key roles, and key relationships. These articles proved to be invaluable in the search for insight and examples to illustrate the principles contained within *The Lincoln Authority*. Abraham Lincoln's Classroom can be found here: *http://abrahamlincolnsclassroom.org/*

Preface

Lincoln's Reputation

Tolstoy, the famed Russian writer, related to Count S. Stakelberg his experience of visiting a tribal chieftain in remote Russia in 1908. After describing his travels, he noticed the chief became very interested when he began to speak of great leaders. The chief asked him to pause until he could call his neighbors and sons to listen.

> "He soon returned with a score of wild looking riders and asked me politely to continue. ... When I declared that I had finished my talk, my host, a gray-bearded, tall rider, rose, lifted his hand and said very gravely:
>
> 'But you have not told us a syllable about the greatest general and greatest ruler of the world. We want to know something about him. He was a hero. He spoke with a voice of thunder; he laughed like the sunrise and his deeds were strong as the rock and as sweet as the fragrance of roses. ... He was so great that he even forgave the crimes of his greatest enemies and shook brotherly hands with those who had plotted against his life. His name was Lincoln and the country in which he lived is called America, which

is so far away that if a youth should journey to reach it he would be an old man when he arrived. Tell us of that man.'"[1]

Tolstoy found Lincoln's leadership resonated to the ends of the earth. A style of leadership, remarkable, not merely for the extent of authority wielded, but for its character—its balance between "strength" and "sweetness" in the words of the Russian tribal chief. *The Lincoln Authority* describes this critical 'balance.'

During my career there was one leader whose leadership was both firm and positive. He mentored others concerning the *exercise of authority*. Since then, in hundreds of client interactions, I have identified and categorized specific leadership actions which either detract from or contribute to the effective exercise of authority.

Leaders today need to add these principles to their practice of leadership, for the majority of employees are not engaged in their work.[2] This represents a significant loss of potential performance. A critical aspect of leadership must still be missing for this lack of engagement to exist—too few leaders know how to exercise the kind of authority which can deliver employee engagement *and* business achievement.

The Lincoln Authority addresses this engagement-leadership gap and conveys ready-to-apply concepts in short, concise chapters, illustrated through examples from the life of Abraham Lincoln.

The Lincoln Authority is a guide to authority, rather than a book about history. Lincoln should be studied and historians, such as Kearns Goodwin, Gienapp, Lehrman, and White Jr., have made it possible for us to know him.

The model of authority explained within *The Lincoln Authority* will help you and your organization to engage employees and more quickly achieve business objectives. It will forever change your practice of leadership.

K. N. M.

1. Introduction

> If Lincoln achieved greatness, he grew into it. Not every individual possesses the capacity for growth; some ... seem to shrink, not grow, in the face of crisis. But to rise to the occasion requires not only an inner compass but also a willingness to listen to criticism, to seek out new ideas.[3]

Lincoln expanded through each new stage of his life. A leader with an increasing ability is inspiring. Lincoln's *firm* and *positive* exercise of authority serves as an indispensable benchmark for all leaders seeking to expand their influence and their practice of leadership.[4] This book is about the exercise of authority—how leaders manage and direct people.

Like Lincoln, you are a leader, or you hope to be one soon. The scope of your leadership may not be as broad as Lincoln's, but as you read these words you are prompted by a similar desire: to grow, learn, and innovate.

As all leaders do, you seek to uphold two main objectives:

1. Deliver results, and

2. Keep every person engaged.

Maintaining an effective balance between these objectives, however, appears to be a challenge. Consider these findings from the 2013 Gallup Report, "The State of the American Workplace"[5]:

- 70% of the American workforce represented themselves as either 'not engaged' or 'actively disengaged'.

- Organizations with higher ratios of engaged to disengaged workers "experienced 147% higher earnings per share (EPS) ..."

- The report concluded, "Managers are primarily responsible for their employees' engagement levels."

Implications:

Organizations accentuate results but may not be instructing managers how to be both firm and positive.

- All leaders could benefit from a practical model of effective and engagement-sustaining leadership.

For 70% of employees to say they are disengaged, the adverse behavior of a small minority of managers must discourage others outside their teams.

- Organizations need to bring every leader's practice of leadership to a baseline.

Organizations with higher ratios of engaged employees earn higher profits than competitors with fewer engaged employees.

- A balanced exercise of authority can raise business performance and employee engagement.

Engagement to Authority

Employee engagement is only one aspect of a larger explanation of Gallup's findings. Engagement levels indicate the health of *individual* relationships between employees and their immediate managers. A program focused solely on raising engagement levels, however, cannot significantly affect business performance because it omits key organizational and operational factors.

The Lincoln Authority moves leaders from employee engagement, an excellent *indicator,* to a *model* which fully explains what goes on inside organizations and describes the actual *skills* leaders need to firmly and positively exercise authority as influential members of a powerful management team.

Benefits

As a leader, if you apply the principles described, you will:

- Wield a degree of influence which will be difficult to overlook. As your team responds quickly and thoroughly to your directives, you will be able to seize opportunities and achieve outcomes in less time and with less frustration. *The Lincoln Authority* will increase the leadership impact of every hour you spend with your team.

- See how each of you contributes to and relies upon your management team peers. Respect *between* leaders will improve and respect *for the entire* management team will also improve.

- Increase your personal influence and your organization's responsiveness. With employee energy more effectively harnessed and directed, this increased agility can mean survival in today's marketplace.

Configured to Apply

Each chapter begins with a historical illustration of the main topic from Lincoln's life. The topic is then defined and pragmatic guidance follows. *The Lincoln Authority* clearly and concisely outlines the four main facets of authority to help you to incorporate them into your leadership practice and impart them to others:

1. Explanation of Authority

2. Essentials of Authority

3. Exercise of Authority

4. Expansion of Authority

Why Lincoln—Manager?

Lincoln remains a benchmark of the exercise of firm and positive authority. Using Lincoln's life as a model prevents distractions which might arise from a more recent leadership example.

The Lincoln Authority is for every leader, from veteran CEO to junior Supervisor because all achieve results by *managing others. The Lincoln Authority* uses the term 'manager' or 'managers' to emphasize this aspect of leadership.

Practical, Powerful

The Lincoln Authority is practical and realistic. It describes the core of what managers do every day—how they exercise authority, give direction, and evaluate results to ensure accountability. *The Lincoln Authority* is a model leaders can follow to increase their influence and make their organizations more powerful.

Let's go. *The Lincoln Authority* is your next step. Read it through and apply the concepts within your practice of leadership. You'll see suggested next steps in the final chapter.

Section One:
Explanation of Authority

Includes:

Explanation:

2. Authority Structure

"Lincoln's problems with Hooker gave him a better understanding of the importance of maintaining a clear chain of command, and he therefore corresponded with his generals less frequently in the second half of the war."[6]

Ineffective, indecisive generals hampered the Union's efforts in the first half of the Civil War, which caused Lincoln to look for new leaders who could lead *and* fight. Perhaps too eager to facilitate decisive action, he agreed to the newly-appointed General Hooker's request to be tasked directly by the President instead of through his military superiors.

Lincoln soon realized this arrangement weakened the authority of those more senior and corrected the situation, resolving thereafter to support and work within the chain of command.

'Structure'?

We're going to describe the authority structure and its individual, operational, and organizational aspects more fully. While employee engagement levels describe how employees *feel* about their managers, the authority structure also describes how a workforce *executes* for their organization.

The following diagram describes the Authority Structure model which includes:

- The relationship between an employee and manager (seated at a desk).

- The relationship between managers and their direct reports.

- How the behavior of any one manager affects other teams and employees.

- The effect of managerial behavior on the willingness of all employees and managers to follow directives and the resulting impact on business performance.

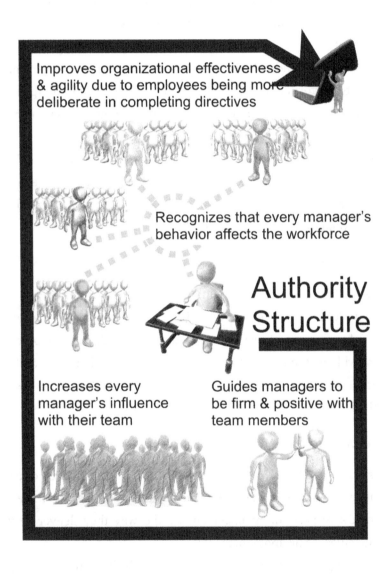

Improves organizational effectiveness & agility due to employees being more deliberate in completing directives

Recognizes that every manager's behavior affects the workforce

Authority Structure

Increases every manager's influence with their team

Guides managers to be firm & positive with team members

Individual

Imagine a *network* of individual work relationships between employees and their immediate managers—this is the 'structure.' These individual relationships are what organizations measure as employee engagement.

As they join, individuals pledge allegiance to the organization, agreeing to perform specific activities under the direction of appointed individuals for the organization's benefit, in exchange for remuneration and/or the opportunity to contribute and personally develop.

Each relationship in this 'structure' is affected by employees' perceptions about their immediate managers and their exercise of authority—whether it is exercised with consistency and respect (and how they feel about other managers as well).

Operational

The health of these work relationships can affect employees' willingness to follow management directives. Operational performance will suffer if, for example, directives are carelessly issued, poorly monitored, or if individuals are not held accountable for expected actions. A strong authority structure means actions consistently flow from issued directives.

Organizational

Lastly, this *network* of work relationships is interconnected across the entire organization. Managers can weaken or strengthen the entire workforce's respect for management by the way they deliver results, cultivate allies, or promote their careers.

For example, if senior leaders go around their direct reports and give direction to junior leaders or employees (as Lincoln initially did with Hooker), it can damage the authority structure because those directed are taught to ignore their managers and wait for senior leaders to become involved. Lincoln eventually learned to work within the authority structure or the chain of command.

As previously mentioned, if one or two managers who treat people poorly are left in place because they deliver results, this extinguishes the passion people have to deliver for the management team and organization.

There are many ways managers can act to either strengthen or weaken the authority structure. *The Lincoln Authority* is a guidebook for managers to follow as they lead within and in support of the authority structure.

Within the 'Structure'

A manager, by definition, is a person under authority who directs others in order to achieve beneficial objectives for the organization. A manager's primary role is to accomplish objectives through subordinates, but not at the expense of the self-esteem of those subordinates.

Technical expertise may be a critical selection criteria and crucial to guiding an area's operation, however, managers, at a minimum, should know how to direct people—to cause actions to occur. This is what organizations expect and need from their managers.

To clarify, a manager gives direction to and evaluates the performance of direct reports. Individuals who give some direction but leave the evaluation of performance to others are not managers since they are not positioned within the organization's line of authority.

Powerless Apart

Experienced managers recognize the support they receive from the 'structure' (as subordinates follow their direction) and the support they, in turn, provide to the 'structure' (as they follow others' instructions). A manager who resolves to work within the confines of the authority structure promotes its safekeeping.

When managers yield to temptation and go outside the authority structure it is never without cost. The aforementioned senior executive who issues directives to subordinates several levels down demonstrates to both management team and workforce that the reporting structure is expendable and can be disregarded when advantageous. The senior manager's action may achieve its immediate purpose, but it will be at the cost of a weakened authority structure, up to and including the executive's own position and authority.

'Structure' Needs Protection

"The first responsibility of a manager is to protect the 'structure'. Without it you can do nothing and you will not be a manager."[7]

Regarding the authority structure's operational impact, it could be compared to a sailboat's sail and rudder: the control surfaces which harness energy and convert it to forward motion.

Without a healthy authority structure, the organization cannot easily harness employee energies or direct activities and the sailboat loses its momentum and steering.

A weak authority structure is evident. For example, when departments seem unwilling or unable to carry out needed activities and employees see no repercussions or when higher-level managers need to step into an area for activities to occur. Employees notice the lack of management oversight, lose respect for management, and lower their performance to the level of enforcement. Engagement and productivity decline until operations barely react to strategic direction.

While this explains the weaker performance of organizations with disengaged workers found in the 2013 Gallup study, building a strong authority structure requires a continual effort to counter what are often typical behaviors. There is something about human nature which continually chafes against even the benign exercise of authority.

There are two reasons for this:

- One, all of us have a built-in tendency to rebel against authority from time to time. Put up a sign telling people *not* to do something and you'll be shocked how quickly people flaunt the prohibition.

- Two, there is always a degree of defenselessness involved with committing to follow someone else's direction as a subordinate.

Taken together, it doesn't take much for any of us to test the resolve of our superiors and see what we can get away with. This is quickly apparent when managerial directives are communicated in a callous, disrespectful manner.

It is fragile.

The authority structure depends on a climate of mutual respect as directives are constantly issued and hopefully followed. Employee enthusiasm (or lack thereof) in following directives does impact business performance. Levels of enthusiasm vary greatly based on the positive (or negative) actions of the organization's management team.

The poor overall levels of engagement indicated in the Gallup study are most likely caused, not by the majority of managers being ineffective, but rather by organizations which permit one or two inconsiderate managers to remain. The negative actions of only a few managers can damage an entire workforce's engagement and commitment to follow directives.

The Lincoln Authority helps managers see and avoid some of the ways they can inadvertently harm their organization's powerful *and* fragile authority structure and weaken employees' respect for management, and their inclination to follow directives. For example:

- When managers make decisions without consulting their subordinates who may have valuable intelligence about the situation.

- When managers fail to consider their subordinates' talents, limits, and preferences.

- When managers criticize or complain about other managers (or their team) to colleagues or in front of employees. This reveals the management team to be a 'team' in name only.

- When managers' actions appear harsh or disproportionate, it can damage employee trust.

- When managers act, speak, and react in a courteous or condescending manner it affects the authority structure as they demonstrate or invalidate respect for direct reports. In 1863, Lincoln demonstrated his humility and respect for regular soldiers as he reviewed sixty thousand soldiers for almost six hours. "He touched his stovepipe hat in a return salute to the officers, but uncovered his head to the soldiers in the ranks."[8]

Building Its Strength

An organization's authority structure, then, is like a person's reputation which takes years to build but can be easily damaged by a few acts of careless behavior. Every managerial action which subverts the authority structure's integrity and fairness weakens its effectiveness and power.

A functioning authority structure is necessary for an effective organization. This atmosphere exists when people are consulted for their ideas and where employees' allegiance is earned daily.

We will now describe five fundamental requirements for building a strong, capable authority structure.

Section Two:
Essentials of Authority

Includes:

Essentials:

3. Authority Delivers Results

British military historian John Keegan wrote, "What Lincoln looked for in his generals was the ability to achieve results without constantly requiring guidance from Washington or reinforcement by additional troops ..."[9]

After replacing a number of generals for inaction and demoralizing defeats, Lincoln found leaders, notably Grant and Sherman, who delivered the results: the victories the Union needed. A mentor once summarized this principle aspect of authority in this way:

"Managers get paid to make things happen. They are not paid simply to give orders."[10]

To direct the activities of others in pursuit of results, the best managers:

Clearly Understand

Managers are more valuable when they spend extra time to understand and communicate the business reasons behind the directives they issue. As they periodically communicate a broader picture in brief summaries, their direct reports become more strategic in their thinking.

Armed with a wider perspective, staff can better adapt tactics to ensure real objectives see visible results. A strategically minded team achieves quickly and distinguishes its manager.

Determine a Course

Leadership requires analytical skill. For more important activities, conditions must be assessed and managers should utilize their staff's collective experience and suggestions as they consider and define what needs to be done. Authority-building managers know the overall objective is to grow the capability of their teams and organizations. They gather information and evaluate options with their teams to gain additional insight and increase commitment to proposed activities.

Involving staff in important decisions doesn't mean you have abdicated your decision-making to staff opinions. The decisions are still yours to make but you create learning opportunities as you demonstrate how to investigate and balance competing priorities before coming to a decision.

Directives:

Proper Action

Directives are correct when appropriate in focus, scale, and priority. They are reasonable even if challenging, realistic given the situation, and attainable given the resources. A 'proper' directive improves both the manager's and the company's standing when it is not given out of selfish, indulgent, or alarmist reasons.

Their successful execution may entail sitting with individual contributors to explain more fully what is expected and how the sequence of events corresponds to your assessment of the situation. Even an organization's president has direct reports who might benefit from such an explanation.

Too often, we assume our direct reports share our experience and insight, so we shorten the explanations which accompany directives. In addition, our direct reports are sometimes reluctant to ask for additional explanation, fearing they will be perceived as 'unaware,' or worse. These two factors—assuming too much and being afraid to ask—can result in easily avoided, reputation-damaging errors.

Effective managers take a few minutes to overview with direct reports the decision, the resulting tactical plan, and any contingencies or factors which should be accommodated or mitigated. Managers should then ask if there is anything else that should be taken into consideration. Taking time with direct reports to ensure everyone is on the same page communicates respect for individuals, gives them freedom to volunteer missing information, and yields more consistent messaging related to the planned activities.

Proper Tone

It may be easy to start the conversation with a direct report with the best intentions while inadvertently using a tone which conveys a lack of trust in their judgment, skill, or intellect.

A directive must be given in a respectful manner in order to motivate people to deliver their best. Even a 'right' order given in a condescending or dictatorial manner damages the authority structure, diminishes trust in leadership, and encourages staff to disengage.

Leaders who deliver directives harshly, mistakenly believe their severe tactics demonstrate strength and power rather than insecurity and a profound lack of appreciation for the potential contributions of others. Effective managers avoid this temptation and grow their organizations by communicating clear directives and sincere respect.

Proper Accountability

Managers who give directives without ensuring their completion only pretend to be leaders. They may give directives but they ignore one of the most vital aspects of managing people: accountability. Those who avoid potential conflict and difficult discussions don't realize the damage they cause to their management peers and their organizations when they don't hold their areas accountable.

Effective managers monitor activities and their impact, not only to ensure the organization receives the expected benefit but also to improve their directive-issuing skills going forward. Accountability discussions should center on what the organization needed to achieve from the not-fulfilled activities.

A manager must follow directives through to their completion to ensure results and then hold people accountable if actions fall short and recognize their success if actions meet expectations. Very few things damage the authority structure more than managers who refuse to hold individuals and teams accountable for achievement gaps.

Likewise, not providing adequate recognition and appreciation when it is warranted can also damage employee engagement and authority. Managers should take every legitimate opportunity to celebrate achievement and extra-ordinary effort. One of the most common reasons individuals cite for leaving organizations is the perception that their efforts were not appreciated.

While both are essential to a strong organization, most managers find it more difficult to hold staff accountable for unfinished directives than to praise them for significant achievements.

Considerations:

Timing

Delaying a decision is really choosing to "do nothing" and is often the worst possible decision. Managers must be able to make decisions with less than perfect information and move on to support those decisions with concrete action. This is another reason why it is so helpful to involve team members in gathering information and evaluating alternatives.

Effective leaders know committing unreservedly to a course of action improves the probability of a successful outcome. Required resources are always easier to allocate to a crisply made, knowledge-based decision. Commitment and adequate resources increase the survival rate of any course of action.

Degree of Importance

The administration of directives is as important as their issue. Managers must oversee actions, from an appropriate vantage point, and gauge their impact. This reinforces to direct reports (and to other employees watching), the significance you place on your directives and your expectation that they be followed through to completion.

How you hold individuals accountable depends on the action's importance. People need to know the core actions which you expect from them so they can distinguish between critical and less-critical actions. We will cover this in more detail later in the book.

For less significant actions which are missed or not achieved, you may only need to verbally tell employees of the discrepancy. Pull the individual aside for a short private conversation soon after the event and tell them what you expected, specifically how their performance missed the mark, and how future directives need to be treated differently to avoid consequences. Provide an opportunity for them to correct their behavior by having the discussion soon after, rather than wait for the individuals' annual performance review.

For more significant omissions related to core-area directives, ask individuals to come to your office or cubical (if private conversations are practical) to discuss the situation. The difference in venue will help employees recognize a more serious discussion. Tell them what you expected, how their performance missed the mark, how this occurrence may be factored into their upcoming assessment, and how future directives must be completed to avoid additional consequences.

Again, do not wait until the annual review. Have the discussion shortly after the incident.

Directives: Achieved

Managers do not give a directive and hope for the best. They first understand the situation, determine a response, decide without delay, communicate with respect, and then monitor expected action for appreciation or accountability.

Operating in this manner, good managers strengthen their organizations by creating a context where instructions are clear, people are consulted, and, most of all, things happen. They work to maximize the organization's capability as they build the authority structure.

Essentials:

4. Authority Maintains Objectivity

> "Beneath a smooth surface of candor and an apparent declaration of all his thoughts and feelings, he exercised the most exalted tact and the wisest discrimination. He handled and moved men remotely as we do pieces upon a chessboard."[11]

Lincoln's focus was the survival of the United States of America. To preserve the Union, Lincoln was willing to employ even questionable political tactics and appoint leaders from various constituencies to secure their backing. While orchestrating support, he never let himself be subject to the will of any group or individual, nor did he ever seek or obtain any benefit for himself.

Lincoln maintained his integrity and objectivity in decision-making. He knew independence from parochial interests was essential if he was to execute his oath of office and win the war.

All leaders need objectivity. Somewhere between the authoritarian's sterile coldness and a friend's affectionate ease is the aloofness every manager requires to be effective. This emotional distance is as essential a part of a manager's equipment as any technology, tool, or strategy.

Essential and a Balance

Managers are placed in authority to execute corporate directives and to impartially deploy resources and evaluate employee performance. You are an agent of management employed to orchestrate activities to benefit the entire organization.

Just as Lincoln's allegiance was purely to his country's welfare, your goal is to serve your *organization's best interests* and to foster an engaged, effective workforce.

You must be willing to promote the corporate good even at the expense of your employees' temporary comfort. As a result, it is not your responsibility to keep employees 'happy.' While being willing to make them 'miserable,' if required in the short-term, you must at all times treat them with respect and consideration.

It is also apparent that this necessary objectivity is constantly tested. Inappropriate gifts and favors bait naïve managers. The politically-minded endlessly strive to influence decisions by building a bridge of friendship to you with the expectation of special treatment.

Balance

A manager who is too distant from subordinates will lack the insight required to optimize activities and effectively deploy employees. People follow distant leaders with a growing frustration, as situations and abilities are continually misread. Lincoln maintained an appropriate distance at all times:

> Edward Duffield Neill, a White House staff member from 1864, described Lincoln this way: "He was independent of all cliques. Willing to be convinced, with a wonderful patience he listened to the opinions and criticism of others."[12]

If managers become 'too close' to their subordinates, it is easier for them to lose respect and try to exploit their relationships—echoing the saying, 'familiarity breeds contempt.' Pulling back to a position of objectivity then becomes significantly more difficult.

Why Friendly is Better than Friendship

Being friendly is good. Being friends is not. Friendship describes a relationship between peers—between equals. People want to be sociable and it is especially easy to be friendly with people who perform their jobs well.[13] Close personal relationships, however, between managers and their subordinates usually look like one of the two following no-win scenarios:

- You ignore your duty to your company and treat an individual as a friend: a manner other than their job performance deserves. In so doing, you violate your obligation, your responsibility to your organization. Your ability to manage is diminished, the expectation of impartial administration is reduced, and the commitment normally given to corporate directives is undermined. You've harmed the authority structure.

- You ignore your relationship and treat the individual in a manner dictated by their performance. Unless there is an unlikely correlation between their perceived performance and their perceived treatment, the friendship will be strained. Cooperation within your department suffers as word of your disloyalty spreads within the organization. Employees lose respect for you *and all management* and the authority structure is again damaged.

This could be summarized in the words of a mentor, "When you become a manager, you have to stop drinking with your folk."[14] This perfectly characterizes the impossible situation of a 'too-close' manager who goes out—as a peer—with the team, then fires one or more team members the following day.

Considerations:

What About Mentoring?

Successful mentoring relationships adhere to this rule as well. The mentor is higher up the organizational structure but *not* in a position of authority over the mentored individual. This way, wisdom and advice can be dispensed from an interested but ultimately *objective* vantage point, preserving the authority structure.

The only exception is a situation where a successor has already been publically announced. The succession plan's achievement then relies on establishing a close mentoring relationship with the senior manager.

Undo a Friendship?

Say you have a manager under your authority violating this rule. Is there a way to undo the damage?

Yes, if it is caught and corrected in the early stages of the relationship. How do you undo a friendship? The remedy may require the removal of the manager in order to preserve the organization's effectiveness. The welfare of the entire organization and its authority structure must be the overriding consideration.

Aren't Teams Equal?

Sports teams are rarely made up of equals. Professional athletes have different abilities and their compensation corresponds to the market value of a position, an individuals' performance potential, and its value to the team. For example, NFL quarterbacks are usually one of their teams' highest paid players because of their role, visibility, and responsibility.

Teams don't require equality, but they do need a common goal, a common fate, and mutual respect. Every person has equal worth and deserves respectful treatment. Not everyone, however, has equal ability or responsibility within an organization. If you are a manager, you have a greater responsibility since you have been granted authority to direct others.

Maintaining Objectivity

On a practical level, maintain a distance but stay informed. Don't relate socially with a specific subordinate or subset of your direct reports, but instead relate to the group. If you find yourself getting too close to one or two direct reports, ask yourself how the individuals and your team would respond if you were to reassign the more familiar ones or lay them off.

In social situations with your team, make your exit before opinions become critical and require you to pointedly defend the organization. Remember, everyone complains; know when to withdraw.

Cultivate a circle of friends outside of those for whom you are responsible. Recognize your position and act objectively to protect your role, your company, your people, and your authority.

Essentials:

5. Authority Represents Leadership

President Lincoln confided to Congressman William T. Kelley, "McClellan ... contrived to keep the troops with him, and by charging each new failure to some alleged dereliction of the Secretary of War and President, had created an impression among them that the administration was hostile to him, and withheld vital elements of success that should have been accorded to him, and which, in some instances, he falsely represented as having been promised."[15]

General George B. McClellan provides an example of poor leadership. At the beginning of the next chapter we will refer to McClellan's failure to perform and refusal of direct orders. Here we emphasize his words and the *position*, relative to the chain of command, from which he spoke.

McClellan vainly, falsely, and shortsightedly complained to his officers and soldiers as a way to "keep the troops with him," to ensure their loyalty to him. As he criticized their collective leadership to his direct reports, he 'positioned' himself *outside* the chain of command. McClellan, a representative *inside* that same command structure, should have kept his troops loyal to the Union, its war administration, and their Commander in Chief.

McClellan chose to 'position' himself as a *victim* of authority rather than an *agent* of authority. He was intensely popular with his army, but at the steep price of his army's morale as well as their respect for and allegiance to their leadership.

McClellan serves as a clear warning to all who like to be popular with their direct reports and staff.

While every leader enjoys delivering good news, managers reveal their true wisdom when they convey difficult or challenging directives and/or decisions from above, whether from a board of directors or senior leadership.

The 'position' managers choose to speak from is far more important than the actual words used. Their choice of 'position' either strengthens the authority structure or sabotages their place within it.

Authority-building managers take personal responsibility and align themselves *with* the company when sharing negative information. An example illustrates this principle:

A Manager's 'Position'

You are a manager within a struggling company. Senior management decides salary increases will be lower than employees are expecting. It is now your responsibility to present this decision to hopeful subordinates. You face a decision regarding this prospective conversation.

You are tempted to say something like, "The raise I thought you all deserved was turned down upstairs and they're only allowing me to grant you this amount."

If this was your choice, you have yielded to the moment. You refused to align with the management of the firm and support their resolution in front of your subordinates.[16] Your 'position'? You have placed yourself *between* the company and your subordinates.

By choosing to speak from this position, you have communicated that you are:

- Not responsible for your subordinates and have chosen not to represent your company to them (effectively removing yourself from the organization's reporting structure).

- A powerless victim of unknown management workings (revealing a lack of influence and giving the impression that you can no longer advocate for them within management).

- Willing to undermine authority by calling into question management's consideration of your area and its employees (and by implication, you) because management *ignored* your 'suggestion'.

- Encouraging your direct reports to appeal to those more senior in the reporting structure

If those senior to you grant meetings to your direct reports, your contribution may not be sought during the discussion, perhaps injuring your authority beyond repair. Your abdication could result in a de facto promotion for your team.

Your subordinates may proceed directly to those above you in leadership, if similar issues again arise. If their visits accumulate, your position will be superfluous since those superior to you will be effectively managing your subordinates for you.

No In-Between

Managers represent the organization to their departments and, in a practical sense, managers are the organization to employees. Managers cannot position themselves as intermediaries between employees and senior management. No such position exists; it has too brief an existence. A manager in this position is ineffective as an agent of policy and must be immediately removed and replaced with a manager who can bring people along in heart, mind, and body to accomplish corporate objectives.

Delivering Difficult Decisions

Managers must align themselves with management *especially* when they personally disagree with the decision. As previously discussed, giving great news from those above you is easy; the challenge is delivering less-favorable decisions.

Effective managers first align themselves and then they can align their teams. Managers must *sell* themselves on the merits of the difficult decision prior to talking with staff. If not, subordinates will quickly identify any reluctance.

Here is the secret: remind yourself of the four (or more) good decisions which preceded this questionable (in your mind) directive. Think about the organization's larger goals as they relate to the decision so you can present a rational, believable argument to your subordinates. Managers who are hesitant or critical negate their own efforts.

Find out some of the details behind the decision if possible. There will be questions and employees will expect you to be aware, to a degree, of the motivation for the decision. Anticipate the concerns from your direct reports and get some answers before meeting with them. A few minutes of preparation will win you increased respect.

Make the case for the company's decision, outline why you think it's a good idea, list specific benefits for the organization, and finally, touch on any tangible benefits for your area.

Whenever possible, leave some of the tactical choices related to the decision's implementation to your direct reports. If they can put their own stamp on the decision, it will appear less imposed and all will benefit from their increased involvement.

Negative Politics

Managers cannot complain about their leadership, their management peers, or higher-level decisions to subordinates.

When complaints go down the chain of command, it damages the authority structure and trust in management. This is what McClellan did to his junior officers and troops, reasoning they would hold him in higher regard if they thought the administration had abandoned his army. Lincoln's two assistants, Nicolay and Hay, considered McClellan's actions "mutinous".[17]

In the best-led organizations, criticism goes up the chain of command while only recognition and appreciation make the return trip.

Organizations need to guard against 'negative' political interference because it is so damaging to authority. Managers must fundamentally believe their organizations' decision-making is impartial and objective (for the most part) so they can effectively convey this belief to their subordinates in order to foster trust.

Politics can be 'positive.' Lincoln exerted tremendous influence, but acted at all times with personal integrity and selfless desire for the organization's best interests.

'Negative' politics is the attempt to influence decisions for primarily personal considerations without putting first the organization's best interests. This shreds managerial trust as decisions are made which make no sense apart from political imperatives. Managers who no longer believe in the overall equity of decision-making cease to be effective agents. Managers and employees disengage to protect their emotions, stow away their passion to perform, and reduce their commitment to act. Inevitably, organizational performance suffers.

One Safe Position

There is only one safe 'position' for managers: it is within the chain of command. Your role exists to represent your organization's management (e.g. board of directors, shareholders, or senior leadership) to your direct reports and all who report to them.

Voice any concerns, respectfully, upward through the chain of command to your board or supervising manager as you advocate for necessary direction, detail, resources, and support for your area of responsibility.

To your subordinates, voice confidence in the direction, decision-making, and leadership of your organization. If you feel you can no longer do this, then you should continue to act as if you genuinely support your leadership while you begin to look for an alternate position.

Regarding a new position, remember most organizations look effectively-run until you begin to learn the details of current activities. The adage, 'the grass always looks greener,' applies here. You may well find similar situations repeated in new environments, so it may be prudent to remain: to advocate for your team and work to promote necessary change.

Essentials:

6. Authority Ensures Accountability

"On November 5th, 1862 Cabinet signed the order to relieve General George B. McClellan of command. Lincoln, after a year of inaction and his repeated refusals of direct orders to move and fight, told Cabinet member and ardent McClellan supporter, Francis P. Blair, he had 'tried long enough to bore with an auger too dull to take hold.'"[18]

General McClellan was ineffective and insubordinate. In most organizations, operational failures are seldom caused by insubordination, as managers cite unforeseen events and broken promises of support to rationalize disappointing results. In this, McClellan had few equals. He blamed circumstances, questionable intelligence reports, and many others for his failures—including his Commander in Chief.[19]

Every time managers and employees fail to complete directives it damages the authority structure, whether the failures are due to poor planning and execution or infrequent acts of insubordination. Every failure, regardless of the cause, requires management action to preserve accountability and authority.

Managers need to be mindful of the issue and oversight of their directives due to the impact of a failure on the authority structure:

> "Never give an order if you do not believe it will be carried out. You may feel you can afford the inevitable loss of face, however, the authority structure should not be forced to suffer erosion due to a collapse in the section for which you are responsible."[20]

Why is protecting the authority structure so important? Let's briefly recap what the authority structure is and how it is affected by directives.

Recap

The authority structure as a network of relationships between all leaders and employees depicts the degree to which the workforce respects its leaders and responds to direction.

Again, an organization *operationally* relies on its authority structure in the same way a sailboat relies on its sail and rudder, enabling the organization to harness the power of its people's talents and translate this energy into forward motion along a desired heading.

Impact of Followed Directives

'Followed directives' are one of the more visible evidences of the authority structure. When employees receive managers' directives and fulfill them, it strengthens the authority structure. These followed directives accumulate over time to weave a 'fabric' which reinforces the authority structure—picture the weave visible in carbon fiber reinforcement.

Extending the analogy, the more consistently employees follow direction, the finer the weave and the higher its strength. Organizations so reinforced can take full advantage of employee skills and respond quickly to external influences. A weak authority structure, however, is like a sailboat with a torn sail and broken rudder. Such an organization, now incapable of capturing and coordinating employee efforts, can be pushed off course by the same forces it should be leveraging.

If followed directives demonstrate the authority structure's proper function, then conversely, every directive which is *not* followed— whether due to it being carelessly issued, received, and/or monitored— weakens the authority structure and therefore undermines the workforce's expectation that directives should be seen through to completion.

In light of this, here are some common directive management situations:

Possible—Achieved

Best-case scenario: Evaluate the results, recognize those involved for their laudable effort, and follow through to completion so other employees can see your appreciation.

Possible—Nearly Achieved

The directive involved important, core activities and was possible. Effort was expended but for reasons outside your team's control the required results did not meet expectations. Perhaps there was assistance promised from another internal area which was not received in time or in sufficient quantity.

Highlight for your team what external forces caused the project to fall short and how you, as management, will take concrete steps to make certain future directives are achievable in order to avoid damage to the authority structure and your reputation.

Possible—Carelessly Received

A reasonable and possible directive involving core activities was issued, but insufficient effort resulted in the directive not being achieved. Perhaps the directive was not received with sufficient consideration or you failed to adequately monitor activities to ensure the directive was completed. Whether due to their neglect or your lack of oversight, any failure to achieve has the potential to weaken the authority structure.

To address the most typical cases and causes, you need only evaluate the causes and conduct remedial problem-solving and process improvement to prevent reoccurrence.

In cases of insubordination which concern core activities, however, your part in the matter may be questioned. If you neglected your responsibility to oversee actions, you may be partially to blame and, to a degree, your employees will know this to be true.

Concede to any part you played in the failure to your team. Admitting this will increase the level of respect your employees have for you, while not admitting it communicates a lack of courage and/or integrity and reduces respect for management (not just you). Your team will give you another chance. A failure to oversee your next major directive, on the other hand, would most likely compromise your leadership.

Then, for sporadic examples of obvious insubordination by direct reports, you must impose some consequence (perhaps even termination) and declare your intention to reference this in the upcoming performance review to protect the authority structure (if those involved are to remain with you). If you, even in a small way, contributed to the situation by not overseeing activities, don't be overly harsh.

If you do not impose consequences, your superiors may have no choice but to impose consequences upon you and include this situation in *your* next review. In a well-managed organization, individual managers should not be able to damage the authority structure which other mangers rely on to support their directives and efforts. Doing nothing is not an option.

Impossible—Carelessly Issued

Your casual attitude regarding the authority structure was demonstrated by carelessly giving an order which could not be achieved. A claim of inadequate information as the cause of your error will only highlight your lack of fitness as a manager. You have demonstrated your inability to your team, for managers gather intelligence before issuing directives and never lightly issue important directives. If repeated, it is now your superiors' responsibility to remove you from your position before the authority structure suffers irreparable damage.

Predicament

Every unfulfilled directive related to significant, core-area objectives presents a predicament. While insubordination is infrequent, any continued lack of progress affects the authority structure and requires a senior management response involving you, your subordinates, or both. In most cases an underperforming manager is replaced first.

The key to building a strong 'weave' of followed directives is to investigate prior to issuing a directive and then monitor events to ensure completion.

As previously mentioned, effective managers involve their team in investigating and evaluating tactical options to bring more eyes to each situation. This reduces risk and as employees participate, they are more inclined to see those plans through to completion.

Your attention to directives will strengthen your influence and increase your team's capability over time.

Essentials:

7. Authority Shows Respect

Illinois Governor John Reynolds described to Attorney Charles Zane a brief encounter with Lincoln on the streets of Washington, "There goes a man I have never agreed with politically, and whom I have always opposed, but I would rather shake hands with him than any man living. I always feel when he shakes hands that he means just what the greeting should indicate, that he is my personal friend and wishes me well."[21]

Lincoln could disagree with others and still earn their esteem and retain their friendship. He maintained the same level of respect for people no matter their background, social class, race, or political viewpoint. Rochester, New York's African-American leader, Fredrick Douglass, said Lincoln was the first leader to speak to him as an equal.

"He was 'the first great man that I talked with in the United States freely,' Frederick Douglass wrote, 'who in no single instance reminded me of the difference between himself and myself, of the difference of color.'"[22]

An organization's exercise of authority is anchored in its leaders' genuine respect for those involved. Every perspective advanced or action prescribed in this book is activated—enabled by leaders who are both firm *and* positive.

Leaders who speak to and treat those they lead with derision or contempt can quickly render the authority structure ineffective and hollow.

To learn from his example, consider three motivations which helped guide Lincoln's positive treatment of others:

Aligned to Self

Rarely has any leader been as 'self-made' as Lincoln. Raised in poverty and instilled with a strong work ethic, he spent only a few years in school. His mother died in his youth and his relationship with his father was strained.[23] Any training in language or business was hard-won through persistent effort.

In spite of this, however, he did not disdain those who came from more privileged backgrounds or those with formal education. Nor did he show contempt for others not gifted with his level of talent, discipline, or intellect. Instead, he warned listeners about the dangers of "setting ourselves up to be better than other people."[24]

Rather than compare his own thoughts and actions with those around him, Lincoln set his own standard to guide his behavior. He sought a realistic view of himself[25]—to stay true to himself and remain worthy of his own respect.

> Lincoln told a friend, "It is my ambition and desire to so administer the affairs of the government while I remain president that if at the end I shall have lost every other friend on earth I shall at least have one friend remaining and that one shall be down inside me."[26]

Lincoln's self-respect and personal standard of behavior directed every interaction and helped him to remain principled and courteous.

Aligned to Influence

Whether as a circuit lawyer, debater, or politician, Lincoln sought to move others toward what was honorable and in their best interests. He saw the considerate treatment of others, not only as a recognition of human dignity but as a prerequisite to the winning over of hearts and minds.

Almost twenty years before becoming President, Lincoln revealed his influence-orientation at a lecture given to the Temperance Society of Springfield, Illinois. Lincoln attempted to advise his religious audience— to improve their efforts to persuade individuals not to drink to excess, in order to safeguard the welfare of, especially less fortunate, families. The Society sought to educate people regarding the evils of alcohol and encourage individuals to sign cards, pledges to abstain from alcohol consumption. Lincoln told them their strategy would be ineffective.

While polite, he chided them for demonizing those who drank too much and for calling *alcohol* evil rather than the *abuse of alcohol* evil. He said all people have appetites, human dignity demands a minimum of respect, and attacks upon this dignity only raise defenses to a height no argument can scale. Lincoln counseled the Society to be less prideful and more gracious in order to reduce defensiveness and render their target audience susceptible to reason.

> "When the conduct of men is designed to be influenced, persuasion—kind, unassuming persuasion, should ever be adopted."[27]

Lincoln believed all humans deserved respectful treatment, which would also make them more open to beneficial guidance.

Aligned to Service

Lincoln, even early, did not set his heart on wealth, power, or popularity. Instead he sought to make a difference and earn others' admiration, dedicating himself to "... being truly esteemed of my fellow men, by rendering myself worthy of their esteem."[28]

Dedication to others can be a powerful, sustaining force.

A successful family practice physician once described how his busy practice lost its allure. Patients had become revenue blocks, scheduled to build toward his financial goals. If a patient didn't appear for their scheduled visit, he was more pleased with his schedule's new-found flexibility. He dreaded coming into his office and even contemplated quitting to search for a vocation which would fulfill him.

During this time, a particularly ill patient missed an important appointment and instead of being relieved, the physician began to be concerned for the patient's welfare. Starting with a few house calls, he adjusted his practice to ensure patients actually appeared for their visits so he and his team could care for them.

This new perspective transformed him. Patients became real people, members of an extended family to protect and help. Joy followed. Now he can't wait to come into his office, his staff's morale has never been higher, and he speaks to medical groups about his new-found passion and joy in serving others.

Lincoln saw his fellow human beings, no matter the cause of their uniqueness, as worthy of his attention and sacrifice of service.

Leaders can learn from the practical ways Lincoln communicated his respect for both his adversaries and associates.

He did not steal credit:

- How discouraging it must be for subordinates to see their unique contributions and novel ideas appropriated by narcissistic managers who value momentary compliments over their teams' long-term effectiveness. Employees soon stop exerting creativity under such conditions which decreases the group's capability and flexibility. News of this dishonesty circulates and reduces respect for management. Lincoln's self-confident spring of fresh ideas meant he didn't have to steal others' innovations. "No person civil or military can complain that he appropriated to himself any honor that belonged to another."[29]

He shared credit with others:

- There are times when the reputations of direct reports need bolstering, whether to encourage them emotionally or to maintain their effective authority—or both. Leaders can lend credit for their actions to others to maintain the organization's authority and collective goodwill. Lincoln once sent an order to tentative General Meade, instructing him to go forward and if successful, destroy the order, and if not, release it as a means of self-vindication. Lincoln cared more about victory than he did about being revealed as the battle's initiator. He was willing for General Meade to receive complete credit for the proposed action.[30]

He was willing to accept the blame for his team members' decisions:

- As leaders guide the large-scale activities of their direct reports, they are always technically 'responsible' for everything that occurs within their jurisdiction. As direct reports develop their abilities, however, issues or errors will naturally arise. Effective managers protect their teams' members from being demoralized by undue external criticism. Lincoln knew accepting blame was an essential aspect of leadership and that it was necessary to create an environment where his cabinet members could grow and become the capable leaders their country needed. Even at the start of his presidency, he often took personal responsibility for Cabinet actions.[31]

He listened attentively:

- Leaders listen to their direct reports to gather situational intelligence and ascertain team member perceptions. Listening is one of the most important ways a leader demonstrates an individual's value, while cutting others off mid-sentence communicates contempt and arrogance. Despite being overwhelmed from his first weeks in office, Lincoln was known as a good listener.[32]

He argued the other side of the issue:

- Lincoln was known to respectfully and fairly argue the positive aspects of the opposite side of whatever position he sought to promote. This takes respectful listening to the next level. Imagine how disarming this practice was to Lincoln's opponents. After presenting their arguments in a balanced and unbiased fashion, no one could accuse him of not listening or considering the alternative position. Leaders can use this technique to affirm similar goals[33], suggest alternate tactics, and prevent disagreements from becoming personal.[34]

He was deliberate in selecting, deploying, or moving individuals:

- It can discourage direct reports if they see their leaders make decisions affecting their careers or expertise without adequate consideration. Due to the potential impact on the authority structure, leaders need to weigh the reasons for a decision and then communicate these reasons, at least in summary, to those affected. As will be discussed in the following chapter, Lincoln was known for taking adequate time to arrive at rational 'people' decisions.[35]

A High Standard

Leaders strengthen the authority structure when they honor those they work with and put their organizations, values, and others first. Lincoln respected others because he truly believed every person to be worthy of respect, deserving of consideration, and that he could learn and grow from every interaction. This belief let him set aside pettiness, advocate for mercy, and not judge others. He served others to earn his fellow citizens' esteem while being true to himself.

The lesson Lincoln offers leaders is that we must look beyond ourselves for the source of our motivation. While it can be daunting to compare motivations and actions with an individual who set such a high, consistent, and selfless benchmark, leaders must progress and a high standard can be a lifetime's pursuit.

Section Three:
Exercise of Authority

Includes:

Exercise:

8. Authority Positions Carefully

William O. Stoddard, an aide, described Lincoln's management as "a persistent effort by him to put each man, as nearly as might be, in the place for which he was best fitted and wherein he could perform the most effective service. If, having appointed any man to an especial [sic] duty, he found him insufficient for it, he was quite willing to transfer him to another."[36]

Every time you select someone to join your team or move a person to an alternate position within your team, it deserves your best exercise of judgment which Stoddard described as Lincoln's "persistent effort." The authority structure is too important to be experimented with due to a lack of consideration.

As a result, authority-building managers have a responsibility *not* to put an individual in a role until you are reasonably satisfied the individual can succeed with your help and guidance. While managers have been assigned team members without adequate consultation, this chapter focuses on decisions you control—the people you select and move.

'People' decisions are significant not only for their ability to weaken or strengthen the authority structure, but also their potential to enhance your reputation, as a demonstrated talent in selecting and positioning individuals is notable.

Rather than expound further on the importance of such decisions, let's shift our attention to practical steps you can take immediately to improve your effectiveness in this critical and visible area.

Evaluating External Candidates

Your daily team interactions provide first-hand insight to guide re-assignment of current team members. Establishing a similar level of confidence for external candidates is more challenging.

With only a few documents and a few interview hours, it can be tough to confidently assess candidates' experience, abilities, and their potential performance and cultural fit. Nevertheless, successful place-ment decisions require you to have a level of confidence regarding how candidates might perform in your organization's positions and situations.

Gathering this intelligence can be problematic. Recruiting firms ef-fectively 'sell' candidates so their information may be suspect to a de-gree. Previous employers are not much help as most usually decline to provide anything beyond employment dates, fearing legal repercussions. Candidate references are positively biased—otherwise individuals wouldn't list them.

Busy hiring managers often compound this problem for themselves when they fail to carve out adequate preparation for even significant interviews, choosing to rely on their instincts—for better or worse.

Even in light of all this, there is a solution. The following behavior-based, interview protocol requires a short preparation time, is dead-on effective, and will make you one of the best interviewers in your organization.

Behavior-Based Protocol

The behavior-based questions recommended here are designed to gather specific information related to the main activities of the position. Only definite questions which address necessary behaviors or skills will provide the information you need to differentiate between applicants.

To be clear, I don't recommend one-size-fits-all, 'canned' behavior-based questions. Some interviewers force candidates to choose between hypothetical situations which have nothing to do with the position being discussed. Unrelated questions will not provide information to help sharpen the dataset you need to select the best individuals. More importantly, they waste valuable time and talented candidates often see them as contrived and manipulative.

The behavior-based questions described here generate valuable intelligence as well as demonstrate your preparation and professionalism.

List 5 Skills/Outcomes

Think about the role in question. List the five most important skills or outcomes required for the job. Examples could be leading a project team, handling customer complaints, expanding sales into new markets, improving a team's performance, or leading a department through an organizational change.

Create Questions

Create at least one open-ended question for each area. More sophisticated roles may require two or more questions per area. The format for all questions is the same: "Give me a specific example from your previous work experience where you ...?" Insert the specific skill or desired action at the end of the question.

Looking for a project manager who can lead the team and at the same time keep company executives informed and involved? Here's your starting question: "Can you give me a specific example from your previous work experience where you led the team and at the same time kept a schedule of successful update meetings with major internal stakeholder groups?"

You get the idea. The goal is a series of questions which reveal candidate experiences related to the position's requirements.

Ask Your Questions

When you meet the candidate, your objective is to wait for the job-related intelligence your questions will provide and not to jump too quickly to a decision. Tell them you will ask them to describe examples from their professional experience related to the position's core behaviors or skills, then ask your open-ended questions.

The tough part is being quiet. Don't 'coach' or help out. Too many interviewers talk too much and consequently learn too little. If a description lacks detail then ask for more. Be willing to allow applicants a few minutes to recall their experiences. If they can't think of an example, they probably lack practical experience in that area.

They will also describe coworkers, executives, direct reports, other departments, and their boss, in addition to the specific actions they think match your inquiry. All great intelligence. If they refer too often to the same example, ask them to describe another.

Ask the same, specific, core-area related, behavior-based questions to each candidate in the same way to make the differences between individuals more apparent. Have those conducting interviews meet briefly between interviews to consolidate their impressions.

Why This Works

People cannot fabricate complex situations fast enough during an interview so they end up speaking, for the most part truthfully, from their experiences.

Benefits

This is not misused time; it's marketing and intelligence. A professional interview sends a positive message to other departments within your firm and to the outside community. You'll learn about real situations candidates were involved in related to what's most important for the position. If they've performed similar tasks in the past, there is a higher probability they can successfully perform comparable activities for you.

> We used this method in a multi-billion dollar organization to help their IT division hire a new Chief Technology Officer. This complex role was evaluated, five key areas were identified, and the five interviewing directors and executive directors were each given two questions per key area to fully address the issues involved.

> After the initial interviews, one candidate's answers to the behavior-based questions showed significantly better previous experience in all key areas. Years later, this Chief Technology Officer was still making an outstanding contribution.

Changing a Direct Report's Role

Considering changing the roles of some of your team members? Use the same basic technique to help them understand what's most important in the new role. This will also help you understand how their previous experiences and inclinations match the position's requirements. Analyze the position, define key behaviors, and evaluate each person's suitability and potential to perform.

'People' Decisions

You should only put someone in a position when you are reasonably confident they will be successful in the specified role. Your ability to successfully select and transition staff increases respect for you and the entire management team.

In contrast, if you do not analyze the role's requirements nor gauge the individual's abilities, or if your decision was subject to political influence, there is an excellent chance the person will fail. The more significant the role, the greater its potential impact on the authority structure.

If the person does not perform you will have damaged the authority structure upon which every manager in your organization relies—their respect for management and their intention to follow direction.

Now you will need to determine how best to remove the person from the role after affording them additional opportunity, coaching, and oversight.

Significant Impact

As you will see in subsequent chapters, there is also an impact as a result of leaving a poorly performing individual in place because it demoralizes those upon which your organization's performance depends. Identify what's most important in the role and use this technique to help you find the right individuals for your team. Competent placement is crucial to a sound authority structure.

Exercise:

9. Authority Guides Clearly

Hay's assistant, William O. Stoddard, described Lincoln's "...vast capacity for work, and also the exceedingly valuable faculty of putting work upon others. He could load, up to their limit or beyond it, his Cabinet officers, generals, legislative supporters, and so forth. He could hold them responsible, sharply; but he never interfered with them, 'bothered them,' at their work, or found undue fault with its execution."[37]

Lincoln set the tone with his prodigious work ethic but many managers likewise work long hours while their teams remain unproductive. What set Lincoln apart was his ability to task individuals to capacity, crisply hold them accountable, stay out of their way, and then not be overly critical. This kept his team fully engaged while maximizing his leverage as a leader.

This chapter focuses on providing clear direction as the foundation of managing a productive team.

Guidance From Skills/Outcomes

As already stated, managers should have, as a fundamental practice, a concise statement of the five most important skills or outcomes required for each role within their authority. This set of what's expected is the starting place for not only hiring but also for guiding employees.

It is especially important to *write* out these five key behaviors/outcomes. Writing them out to present to someone, whether an applicant or an employee, forces you to make choices, rank alternatives, and define activities until you're satisfied.

Why Five?

In practice, more than five priorities portray a fragmented agenda whereas three is too few to paint a complete picture of what's essential.

As further justification, your five fingers enable a firm grasp on everything you interact with in your environment—'five' is a proven number.

Will more priorities improve the agenda's resolution? A team responsible for the performance management of many thousands of government employees told me how they evaluate managers based on 37 different priorities. I asked, "When leaders focus attention on one priority do they sacrifice performance on others?" They admitted managers were frustrated by contradictory priorities, but since they believed the sophisticated system impressed senior management, there were no changes planned—in spite of the negative impact on engagement.

A strategic outline with five priorities can be more easily communicated which will improve the likelihood that employees will internalize and act upon your agenda. Employees will welcome your definition and find it liberating whether or not they consider elements on the page daunting or even slightly out of reach.

Most managers are not candid enough with staff about what they want from each role and, due to more urgent tasks, put off the short time required to prepare role requirements. Authority-building managers invest this time and don't leave their direct reports to sort out for themselves what's important; it's too significant an opportunity to help staff see a broader picture of how their roles support the organization. In addition, individuals feel respected when their managers take time to guide their contribution.

Employees Look for More

Ex-Chairman and CEO of General Electric, Jack Welch, conducted an ad-hoc survey of employees and bosses while being interviewed by Dr. Henry Cloud at a largely attended leadership conference.[38] After telling the audience that managers have no right to lead if their employees don't know where they stand, Welch started his informal survey.

He asked those attending with their immediate boss to raise their hands. Thousands of hands when up. Jack then asked those same people to leave their hands up if they *didn't* know where they stood with their boss. The vast majority of those hands stayed up, demonstrating a need for better guidance and feedback. Jack suggested managers look around, take note, and address the deficiencies.

An example can highlight the importance of guiding employees' contributions.

> A client once delayed promoting his 'Acting' General Manager to the position of General Manager despite two years of exceptional effort in the 'acting' role.
>
> I asked the company president why he hadn't promoted the individual. "He's an excellent operational manager, but he doesn't display the sales orientation I expect from a general manager," he said.
>
> I asked what sales-related activities he thought were missing. He replied, "A general manager would regularly contact our twenty largest customers." Probing further, the president believed a

lunch with one of their twenty key customers each month would maintain these important relationships.

I asked this president if he had ever told the acting general manager about his expectation. "No. He's doing such a good job in other areas; I didn't want to discourage him."

The president *assumed* a potential general manager would just *know* what was required. Granted, the operation-oriented 'Acting' General Manager would probably be a little out of his comfort zone until he got used to these meetings. *The business, however, needed this activity to prosper and grow.*

I revealed to the 'Acting' General Manager the real reason his promotion had eluded him. Since my organization was contracted to help improve the company's strategic execution, I told him his bonus would now be dependent, in part, on arranging at least one key-account lunch each month and mentioning the lunch appointment in his monthly report to the president. The entire conversation took less than two minutes.

Though he had never done it previously, this clear accountability (with a link to a pre-existing bonus calculation) changed his behavior—but not his nature. For the next 24 months he didn't miss a lunch with at least one major sales account. Some months he even managed two lunches.

His more-reserved nature worked to the company's advantage as he listened to clients' concerns and then made corresponding operational adjustments. This thrilled clients, created opportunities, and increased sales.

There are several lessons here:

Assuming Is Not Guiding

The president assumed the 'acting' general manager should *know* what was required for such a role in their business situation. The president was looking for a 'perfect' person to perform this role, one who would not require direction from him. I suggested holding the 'acting' general manger accountable would be easier than trying to find a more 'instinctive' general manager. This all too common perspective damages business performance and employee engagement. Everyone deserves to see their leadership's guidance in a statement for their specific role.

Requirement Over Personality

It is probably true that the reserved, operationally-minded, 'acting' general manager's personality wouldn't naturally lead him to regularly lunch with key customers. The reality is, however, the business needed the behavior to succeed. Don't be quick to adjust a role's deliverables to the personalities of those currently involved. Different personalities strengthen your team. Specify what you think is critical and help direct reports picture how these priorities should be reflected in their ongoing behaviors and activities.

Business Needs

Rather than attempting to tailor necessary activities every time personalities change within your team, specify the actions you and your organization need to see within each role. Create individual accountability for these strategic behaviors in spite of any perceived 'natural bent' or personality 'fit'. You will be surprised how your team strives to meet expectations as they see their contribution valued. As it turned out, the 'acting' general manager's *quiet* personality actually suited the newly-implemented, strategic requirement.

Observable Actions

The higher you go on the organizational chart, the less measurable are individuals' behaviors. Expense records could never indicate the strategic value of specific monthly lunches over others. The regular key account lunch was an observable behavior made visible by requiring the 'acting' general manager to list any key account lunches on his monthly report to the president. The president need only read the report to see if the activity was continuing. Only one other mechanism was needed to activate this change in behavior.

Personal Accountability

My communication to the 'acting' general manager was accompanied by a change in individual accountability: the new link between the monthly key account lunches to the president's semi-annual determination of the 'acting' general manager's bonus. Exactly *how* the president would factor or weight the monthly key lunch compared with a multitude of other activities the executive performed was neither discussed nor defined.

The listing of key account lunches on each monthly report to the president would now be one consideration within the individual's bonus calculation. This *alone* moved the key account lunch from the list of *'what would be nice to do'* to the list of *'what I must be sure to do'* in the 'acting' manager's mind. Without personal accountability, suggested actions remain *suggested* rather than *acted upon*. A separate incentive, however, is generally not needed.

Many organizations make matters worse when they 'bolt-on' an incentive as a quick fix for one issue only to find their 'fix' creates multiple other problems and further damages engagement.

The same effect could have been accomplished by linking notification of key account lunches to the 'acting' general manager's yearly evaluation and raise calculation. The real requirement: to make the activity accountable.

Accountability Guides

Many leaders resist the suggestion that employees generally require personal accountability to change their activities. While participating in a client's company retreat, I reiterated this principle to both staff and managers when discussing a long-standing issue. The president disagreed and declared, "No, I have the right people, and they will do what's right (without any accountability adjustment)." There had been no change for years in spite of their leader's frequent admonitions. Months after the retreat, the president finally changed employees' personal accountability to effect the long-sought change in behavior.

Some leaders believe their direct reports will respond as they do to verbal suggestions (without accountability). This is because most leaders are 'value-guided' while most employees are 'environment-guided'.[39]

Value-Guided

'Value-guided' individuals execute well due to their internal, positive, service-oriented motivations. *Few in number*, this well-intentioned group responds to verbal direction because they care and want to please, and with this orientation they are often promoted to management. Hard-wired in this way, they are flummoxed by employees who don't respond as they would to the same stimuli.

Environment-Guided

Most employees are 'environment-guided.' These individuals *primarily* respond to the work environment and therefore seek to maximize personal benefit out of the environment their organization's leadership has constructed. 'Environment-guided' employees respond to clear, *accountable*, formal direction. They look for leadership to encapsulate what's important into the structures which motivate their daily choices.

To guide this employee type, prepare written role priority summaries and ensure accountability for required actions. They will then process this information based on its personal impact, and in most cases, begin to execute them immediately.

Guidance Means Impact

Lincoln knew human nature and mentored others with this reality in mind. Lincoln's assistant Nicolay said, "I used to hold that an action could be pure, disinterested, and wholly free from selfishness; but [Lincoln] divested me of that delusion. His idea was that at the bottom of these motives was self."[40]

Authority-building managers recognize that individuals need personal accountability to generate consistent action. Leaders are not frustrated by this truth: they ensure critical role activities are accompanied by an incremental change in accountability to ensure achievement and protect the authority structure.

Exercise:

10. Authority Evaluates Performance

> M. T. Owens, military historian, stated, "Lincoln never let sentiment or his personal opinion of an officer get in the way of his assessment of the officer's military potential."[41]

Lincoln knew the Union needed to develop its military potential quickly to match the South's well-trained military leaders and then bring the war rapidly to a favorable conclusion. With this as his goal, he sought to set aside personal considerations in the evaluation of any officer's military capability.

Lincoln, Grant, and Sherman and a perhaps a few other senior leaders followed this precept while many of the Union's military command let selfish ambition and bickering damage their cause.[42]

To impartially evaluate performance, managers must separate issues from individuals to maintain team spirit and safeguard the authority structure.

Assessing Performance

Here are some guiding principles for objectively assessing individuals based on their job performance:

Core Behaviors/Activities

The foundation of objective performance assessments are the sets of five core behaviors/objectives you developed for each role. With it, managers have a solid framework upon which to build an accurate picture of performance. Without it, they lack an objective standard by which to gauge individuals' contributions, making it easier to be influenced by personal, political, and non-performance-related issues.

Their Contribution

In today's connected environment with shared and team-based activities, it is rare for an individual to control enough of a major project to hold them solely accountable. If managers try to base assessments purely on individuals' directly-attributable achievements, it can distort the picture of their contribution and give too much significance to smaller personal projects and too little to individuals' main activities.

It is frequently more helpful, and much easier, to evaluate the behaviors associated with the five key aspects you identified and ask yourself, "Did the individuals *contribute* to the team's results? Did they consistently or inconsistently support the team's efforts for a specific core behavior, activity, or objective and to what degree?"

Professional, Not Personal

As mentioned in chapter 4. Authority Maintains Objectivity; managers must keep some emotional distance and resist becoming too familiar so they can deal impartially with direct reports and not allow personal or political considerations to influence assessments.

A mentor stated, "When managers treat people in any manner other than is justified by their job performance, it damages morale and weakens the authority structure."[43]

No Surprise Discussions

You have failed as a manager if, during an assessment discussion, your employee looks at you and says, "But why did you wait until now to tell me this?" When employees are surprised by their managers' assessment comments it is due to the manager's lack of courage, coaching, and consideration.

Lincoln, though immensely patient, was still forthright enough to tell difficult individuals, such as the pompous McClellan, where they stood in his assessment.

> Lincoln told McClellan: "I wish to call your attention to a fault in your character—a fault which is the sum of my observations of you, in connection with this war. You merely get yourself ready to do a good thing—no man can do that better—you make all the necessary sacrifices of blood and time, and treasure, to secure a victory, but whether from timidity, self-distrust, or some other motive inexplicable to me, you always stop short just on this side of results."[44]

Lincoln's summary, given months before McClellan would ultimately be replaced, defined him succinctly, fairly, and with grace. Lincoln also plainly pointed out his main weakness, hoping it would lead to self-correction and improvement. Even after receiving an accurate picture of himself from someone with only his best interests at heart, McClellan continued to blame others.[45] We would all benefit from a personal assessment such as the one Lincoln provided McClellan.

Everything said in an assessment should have already been raised with your employees in at least one of your periodic coaching discussions—as soon as practical after you became aware of any suspect behavior or insufficient activity. This is fair and gives employees an opportunity to take corrective action and rise to your expectation prior to their next assessment.

Objectively, not Financially

Some managers attempt to justify a lower salary increase for employees by collecting examples of poor achievement or behavior and not discussing them with employees during the year. Perhaps they seek to give the incremental payroll amount to another employee who is more worthy or more difficult to disappoint at the time salary increases are announced.

Distorting assessments for budgetary purposes converts performance evaluations into financial manipulations. Employees will eventually find out, resent their treatment, and reduce their trust in management. Assess employees against the core behaviors identified for each role.

Resist 'Bell Curves'

Similar to manipulations of assessments for financial reasons, this practice has managers rank direct reports along a 'bell curve' rather than against the objective standards of core behaviors/activities you've developed by role. Managers classify some employees as best, most as acceptable, and a few as poor performers, as candidates for dismissal. This technique mistakenly assumes team members comprise a 'normal' population in statistical terms, and that managers cannot hire well, mentor well, and that periodic, forced pruning is necessary to ensure a productive workforce. This assumption of incompetence is a slight to professional managers and their well-chosen and mentored team members.

There will always be differences in performance between individuals. Your assessments must reflect only this to preserve the authority structure.

Resist Political Influences

Stand your ground when faced with anyone who asks you to abandon your responsibility to objectively assess employee performance, whether due to personal dislikes or undeclared agendas. Your ability to harness the energy of your team is directly related to their trust in your objectivity. Refuse, at least, on the grounds of continued productivity and, if unsuccessful, pursue an alternate position.

Beware of Systemic Factors

Of all the influences which can keep you from objectively assessing the performance of direct reports, systematic reasons are the hardest to see. They can affect anyone in any position—from company leader to everyday employee.

Imagine you are preparing for the performance discussion with an employee who achieved less-than-expected results. The role in question has already consumed a series of promising candidates and is beginning to look like a revolving door.

Rather than the poor performance being the employee's fault, the cause is more likely to be the position itself. Underlying mechanisms or factors may well make the role impossible to perform. These reasons are often too 'near' for those more familiar to recognize, likely having been in place for an extended period or installed by an untouchable person, such as an owner or political favorite.

When we see failure, humans are programmed to first blame individuals rather than identify below-the-surface, systematic pressures which generate contradictory demands and grind participants down. Our tendency to fault individuals rather than the system in which they operate is called the Fundamental Attribution Error—first recognized and named by Lee D. Ross from Stanford University.[46]

Stop the process, reevaluate the position and realign its demands before assessing the current individual. You may need to get outside assistance if you can't identify the systemic issues at play within the role.

In researching the cause of a difficult role, you should start by looking for contradictory pressures among components which affect employee behavior. I described the four main elements in this 'reinforcing structure' in a previous book.[47] They are:

- Reporting structure;
- Performance measures;
- Employee evaluation (and promotion-causing) criteria; and
- Rewards, incentives, and employee recognition.

After examining these four structures, then begin to evaluate and resolve conflicting expectations.

Once you've simplified and made real adjustments to your 'reinforcing structure', give the employee another chance to succeed and assess them again after a number of months.

Key Aspect of Engagement

The ability to be objectively assessed by their immediate managers is a significant aspect of employee engagement. Few things can more quickly enhance or erode the authority structure.

During the year, meet informally a couple of times for a few minutes and let your direct reports know how they are doing, especially if you think there has been an exception in their typical performance. This gives them an opportunity to make mid-course corrections and rise to your expectations.

Nothing you say should ever really surprise a person in a formal assessment if the individual is reasonable. Affirm what's positive and caution them about what's not. It's an important part of why you're in a place of authority.

Exercise:

11. Authority Interferes Cautiously

> "Lincoln did not like to intervene in the details of military or naval operations. He was no micromanager....He defined the objective and allowed his subordinates to define the means they would employ to achieve it."[48]

A demanding executive officer, Lincoln made clear what he wanted to achieve, and increasingly realized he should not interfere with his direct reports' exercise of authority. He knew his actions could affect his military's willingness to follow the directives of all those under his command.

Lincoln visited Fort Stevens while it was still under attack and stood on a wall looking in the enemy's direction even as a soldier near him fell from rebel sniper fire. Lincoln's lack of concern exasperated Secretary of War Stanton, for both knew an assassination would invigorate the rebels. After a short discussion about whose command was most senior, the fort commander sent an officer to inform his Commander in-Chief of his intention to forcibly remove him if he didn't immediately come down.

Lincoln said, "And you would do quite right, ... you are in command of this fort, and I should be the last man to set an example of disobedience."[49]

Lincoln believed it was important to respect others' authority. Managers must guard the everyday practice of authority within the chain of command by working within it, as Lincoln did. He protected it from both external and internal influences, and resisted any temptation to interfere.

External-Internal Influences

External

Leaders, whether junior or senior, will occasionally be approached by outside individuals in an attempt to gain information or influence ongoing actions. Interference might come from activist board members looking to support a proposed project or from peers hoping to distract senior leadership from their area's poor performance by finding something amiss in your area. Outside influences can be a distraction.

Make it clear to those outside that your area's information will be provided promptly and willingly to support the organization's objectives, but requests for information and suggestions for activity changes should come through you. You need to be seen by those outside and inside your area of responsibility to 'have the backs' of your direct reports and all those who report to them. In effect, you are your area's 'fort commander' to your 'Lincolns'; and directives, requests, and suggestions should all be routed through you so that you can remain aware.

External criticism is challenging. You cannot be seen as too willing to pacify criticism from other areas and especially from senior leaders you want to impress. This can give your direct reports the impression your personal political interests outweigh your loyalty to them and that you might seem willing to suspect their motives and activities when expedient. This would injure the authority structure, your direct reports' trust, and diminish their wholehearted confidence in—and enthusiastic execution of—*your* directives.

Instead of encouraging your staff to invent, experiment, and lead quickly and decisively, an over-attention to outside criticism will teach them to act slowly, cautiously, and second guess your instructions to protect themselves against the disapproval they believe you will again entertain. Managers, too concerned with internal politics, sacrifice the focused, productive team they need to accelerate their success.

Workforce Benefits

The organizational impact of managers who courageously resist yielding to negative political influence is hard to appreciate unless you consider how those working under such authority feel every day. They come to work fully engaged and single-minded, thinking only about how they might best execute the directives issued by their leaders, knowing those same leaders will deal with outside influences and protect their direct reports' interests.

These managers create a fear-free, high-engagement environment where direct reports believe their contributions will be assessed objectively and outside influences will remain secondary.

A non-political environment is so refreshing—and productive. Even these leaders may not fully realize the way their behavior positively affects their staff.

> I once met with an outstanding leader the day he announced his resignation within his large organization—triggered by a senior management personnel decision he could not support. Due to his loyalty to his present employer, he had cultivated no prospects for future employment.
>
> Some among his very few confidants suggested he stay on while looking for a suitable position. He could not. Following his own

high standard of integrity, he chose to leave rather than risk being seen as anything less than totally committed to the organization's senior leadership.

What surprised him was the reaction from his direct reports; their level of dismay caught him off guard. His leadership, a demonstration of firm and positive authority, created exactly the type of confident, focused, and productive environment discussed here. His direct reports' apprehension rose as they realized their next executive officer may not operate in the same protective and, ultimately, productive manner.

It is especially important for an organization's most senior leaders to set an example of respecting authority, as Lincoln did at Fort Stevens. They will be rewarded with the corporate productivity and performance their shareholders seek.

Internal

Just as managers need to protect their areas from outside interference, they also need to prevent their direct reports and staff within their chain of command from criticizing and fighting amongst themselves and their divisions or departments. Whether caused by divisional rivalries or individual bullying, you must quickly address any contrary provocations and work to preserve the climate of mutual respect needed to maintain effective authority.

Lincoln endured the self-promotion and disloyalty of Salmon Chase[50] due to his astute handling of the Treasury Department and his ability to continue to fund the war effort. When Chase's negative actions had so damaged his reputation and support among the Cabinet, however, action became necessary. Lincoln accepted one of Chase's letters of resignation and then graciously appointed him to the Supreme Court.[51] Even in dealing with a troublesome direct report, Lincoln never let personal feelings weaken his continued respect and objective appreciation for those with whom he labored.

Personal Interference

Without a substantial reason, if you interfere with properly functioning areas under your direct reports' authority you will weaken the authority structure. To illustrate this point, here are a few examples of temptations to resist:

Rewrite Agreements

- Resist the urge to modify agreements mid-term, such as incentive programs and sales compensation schemes. While it is wise to put a time period on these types of agreements to allow adjustments based on market and business changes, rewriting them mid-term can be interpreted as breaking faith with your workforce. It will reduce their trust, weaken their engagement, and erode their intention to fulfill directives.

Focus on Immediate Results

- Resist the temptation to mortgage future viability for immediate profitability. Advocate for ways to support both short-term and long-term growth despite continued pressure for immediate results. When organizations oscillate between tactics rather than work for sustained growth, it can discourage talented staff whose longer-term growth ideas are continually shelved for urgent outcomes.

Tinker with Winners

- As leaders take on increasingly senior roles, their authority often extends beyond their original expertise. They need to leave their previous areas alone if they are performing adequately. If they don't, those directing their initial areas can sometimes be overly scrutinized. This may be caused by a leader's desire to jealously revisit past accomplishments or a wish to avoid new responsibilities by staying involved with familiar minutiae, believing this creates an illusion of competent oversight. Managers need to mentor subordinates and set an example by focusing on increasingly fresh responsibilities as their direct reports progress.

Productive and Positive

Effective managers display confidence in those who execute well and encourage others who can't be coached to adequate levels of performance to take more realistic roles—even those outside the organization.

Wise managers reject political interference and seek to make decisions based on merit and the organization's best interests. They know they will improve effectiveness and responsiveness if they protect their areas and let direct reports exercise their own authority.

Exercise:

12. Authority Prunes Protectively

Lincoln appointed General-in-Chief Henry W. Halleck, who started well as "a master of military technique, adept at moving troops and supplies."[52] By 1864, however, historian Craig L. Symonds wrote, "Lincoln had long since concluded that for all his theoretical knowledge, Halleck simply lacked the temperament to give orders. Halleck offered innumerable suggestions but almost never issued an unequivocal order; he simply did not want to command."[53]

For General Halleck's role, Lincoln probably considered the most crucial skill 'the ability to decisively issue clear, crisp commands.' While Halleck excelled at much, Lincoln desperately needed a leader more than an advisor. The Union's field command had floundered without direction, costing lives and wasting resources. The impact of Halleck's deficiencies accumulated until the damage caused outweighed the value contributed and Lincoln removed him.

Leaders face the same calculation today. You have coached and given multiple opportunities for improvement but you have seen enough and the time has come.

Proceed Carefully

The reluctance most managers feel about dealing with performance issues acts as a protection, of sorts, for employees. The leadership objective is always to manage expectations and performance to avoid such outcomes.

The information in this chapter should not be considered legal advice. Human Resources professionals should be consulted as you consider pruning a non-performing individual. The purpose here is to highlight the impact on the authority structure when you, and ultimately your organization, decide to remove a team member.

Respect Preserves Trust

How you proceed communicates a great deal to others. No matter the cause of the termination, respect is still the order of the day—even if the individual, due to singular circumstances, may not, in your mind, deserve the typical approach.

Your decision to treat all with due consideration will strengthen the authority structure, your reputation, and your organization's standing. This is especially true for those—within and outside your organization—who will hear about your decision but will never know the details due to privacy considerations.

Your Perspective is Apparent

Once your *doubt* has formed into a *decision*, it is too late to turn back. You have no choice but to make the necessary preparations and proceed.

Daily actions and language convey your confidence, or lack thereof, in team members. Any hesitation will reveal itself in the way you delegate and follow up on directives. You will unconsciously favor more reliable resources and involve others to ensure adequate outcomes where ordinarily the individual alone would suffice.

Your people are observant; they know the work and they know you. A delay can communicate that job performance is no longer as crucial. An erosion of confidence or trust in you affects the authority structure and employee engagement.

A crisp, clear decision strengthens your team's performance and frees the exiting employee to pursue a position better suited to their gifts and abilities.

No Surprises

As in other job performance discussions, no employee should ever be shocked by the conversation or decisions (unless the individual lacks self-awareness to a remarkable degree).

Unfortunately, I've seen long-term employees terminated for *performance* without having ever received negative feedback. A major university terminated a controller after years of positive performance appraisals. When the senior finance executive handed the controller the termination package, he said quietly, "You never did what I wanted you to do." It's as though the university's finance leader wanted to keep the definition of 'good performance' a secret.

Authority-building leaders hold periodic, plain discussions with employees about core skills, expectations *and* deficiencies, and give opportunity to modify activities. This fulfills leaders' organizational responsibility to actually 'manage' people in order to bring job performance in line with business needs.

Individuals are removed when their job performance and/or their personal behavior significantly affects their team and the organization.

Performance Related

The individual's performance has been reviewed, your remediation efforts and clear behavioral expectations have failed to yield sufficient results, and now you believe your team's performance is being held back.

Nothing here, however, is a surprise. You've done your homework and considered the impact of the underlying mechanisms: the structures and expectations which may compromise a role's potential for achievement. You've taken adequate time to consult with your superiors, peers, and the Human Resources professionals available to you. You are most fortunate if these discussions remain completely confidential. If word has leaked, proceed without delay.

Behavior Related

Here, an employee's negative action(s) have violated policies, norms, or regulatory requirements, perhaps the result of an incident which cannot be ignored.

Investigative efforts to uncover what transpired may yield fewer details than you wish. Employees are usually reluctant to divulge negative information for fear of injuring peer relationships, career prospects, and/or reputations. Whistleblowers are often poorly thought of within an organization. Talk to multiple witnesses and, if possible, consult with your Human Resources department. Document and confirm any verbal instructions given to you about the situation and how you are to proceed.

Collect the required information and guidance at a pace which corresponds to the situation's seriousness. Respond too quickly and you risk being seen as impulsive—too willing to believe reports which may not have been adequately verified. Too long a delay and you may be perceived as indecisive and hesitant—a detriment to both your career and the health of the authority structure.

Pruning for Growth

Pruning your team should be done carefully, progressively, and with the best interests of your team and its performance in mind. You will reinforce to your team the importance you place on delivering results and supporting others. When you proceed respectfully, it demonstrates your professionalism and leadership. Both your decision and the manner of its implementation will strengthen the authority structure.

Section Four:
Expansion of Authority

Includes:

Expansion:

13. Authority Achieves Visibly

"Public sentiment is everything. With it, nothing can fail; against it, nothing can succeed."[54]

Lincoln used a variety of means to secure public support for his administration, for their activities, and the war effort. Even before his election, Lincoln used his speeches knowing newspapers would publish the texts to plant his vision in peoples' minds. He tailored messages to their intended audiences; his pivotal Cooper's Union speech in sophisticated New York was rational, researched, unemotional, and intellectual, far different from the folksy anecdotes and analogies so characteristic of earlier stump speeches and circuit court proceedings.[55]

To refute those advocating compromise with the South, he sought to remind people of what was at stake and, unable to leave Washington, sent letters to be read aloud by others. To ensure the Union's supply of funds and soldiers, he met with and gave appointments to people from various geographic regions and ethnic groups. He believed emancipation was morally right and would increase enlistments to speed victory. To allow time for the public's viewpoint to mature, however, he progressively disclosed his thinking and intentions.[56] To support the war and safeguard the nation, Lincoln managed public perception.

While only senior leaders set their organizations' strategic direction and relay it to the workforce, every effective manager knows the importance of cultivating their organization's view of their area and its activities.

To help you establish a positive perception of your area and secure tangible resources, here are some practical suggestions for communicating your team's accomplishments in a way that strengthens the organization and its authority structure.

Is Promotion Necessary?

Organizations are complex. Boards of directors and other senior leaders constantly divide their attention between external changes and concerns and internal issues and allocations. When their focus *briefly* alights on your area of responsibility, you want them to see fresh evidence of a well-led and well-run group. In contrast, a few notable failures can form a persistent, negative narrative which can be difficult to overcome.

To ensure management esteems your team:

- Build a string of smaller successes, and

- Message these successes constructively, together with other team accomplishments, as examples of the *organization's* prowess.

A String of Successes

Why small? Wouldn't leading longer and higher-value projects bring increased visibility? Perhaps. Leading strategic projects may be required at times in your career, but long projects involve higher risk as external and internal forces affect execution. Your career can get sidetracked by unrealistic expectations long before you can marshal sufficient resources and achieve project milestones.

Small projects have several advantages. Compared to larger projects, they are easier to explain and justify to other senior leaders, making any required cooperation easier to obtain. In addition, the faster learning cycle improves organizational understanding and allows corrections to be made before the next wave of contained projects.

Given short attention spans and rapid industry changes, smaller projects rise above the noise of everyday activities. They are a career's best friend.

Quarterly Projects

Break down larger projects and improvement objectives into short-duration, well-defined sub-projects. Keep editing the scope until each can be initiated and completed within 90 days or less. Closely frame each mini-project's purpose, listing only a few objectives with benefits which will spill over to other areas.

Rather than hold separate project meetings, add project updates to your area's regular team meetings to prevent projects from expanding in scope. Invite representatives to contribute as needed. Obtain any required assistance from other areas in one-on-one meetings outside your regular update meeting.

To keep senior leaders informed, prepare a project update for corporate management meetings. Inform them of the project's successful start, its schedule and objectives, the project's value to the organization, and especially how it will benefit those present. As projects conclude, outline the benefits realized and describe how the organization has supported the project.

Visible appreciation for assistance makes future cooperation progressively easier to obtain. A string of completed projects and a well-functioning area are the foundation of your team's reputation. The next step is to ensure your organization takes notice.

Internal Marketing

To ensure your team's efforts are recognized, you need to *market* their accomplishments across your organization. It is no longer enough to quietly and effectively manage an area, even an important one. You must intentionally foster your team's perception within your enterprise.

Not Against, But Within

Your goal *cannot* be to highlight your area's strength and competence *against* other areas' weakness and incompetence. This would significantly damage the authority structure and reduce cooperation.

The purpose of messaging your area's successes *within* the organization is to:

- Showcase examples of successful projects aligned with strategic goals as proof of the *organization's* advancement toward its goals.

- Appreciate the support received from other areas; describe how it contributed to the project's success—how their assistance resulted in a 'win'.

Successful projects communicated in this manner strengthen the organization's respect for management, cooperation within management, and perception of achievement.

This authority-building messaging can even help to offset less effective organizational tendencies when organizations unconsciously nurture behaviors which weaken authority. For example, when senior leaders ignore competently-run areas and focus attention on 'diving catches'—where poor managers 'dive' in to address emergencies caused by their inaction and/or incompetence. When senior managers only notice and reward the extra effort, rather than investigate the emergencies' root causes, good managers disengage and lose respect for management.

AUTHORITY ACHIEVES VISIBLY

AUTHORITY ACHIEVES VISIBLY

AUTHORITY ACHIEVES VISIBLY

Some managers appear not to actually have a team, due to the way they take personal credit for their team's performance. Lincoln earned his co-workers' respect and allegiance by giving credit away for successes, taking responsibility for his own actions, and also assuming shared responsibility for his team members' mistakes.[57]

Sharing credit builds engagement and heightens the sense of contribution employees long to feel, while stealing credit destroys employees' trust in management.

Your Organization's 'Channel'

Pay attention to how others in your senior management team communicate, be it an in-person presentation, one-page project summary, company newsletter article, and/or circulated report. Senior leaders showcase their favored methods in their communication efforts and this programs the organization over time to receive information in this way. Adopt these techniques to message your team's achieved milestones and project completions.

Message Periodically

Messaging too frequently on partially completed, smaller projects can appear presumptuous, attract criticism, and weaken support from peers. Bi-monthly or quarterly updates may be preferable depending on the pace of your organization's culture. You must walk a balance between ensuring the organization is aware of your team's accomplishments and the appearance of trumpeting every action.

Message Focus

Your communiqués should reflect a succinct view of the organization's direction and the link between current activities and strategic, long-term objectives. Leaders can sense direction, articulate it clearly, and persuade others to join in pursuit. Distinguish yourself by highlighting how your team's recent accomplishments contribute to the organization's goals.

Message Team

As previously stated, your marketing effort must emphasize your team's accomplishments and how other areas joined in these achievements by supporting your team's actions. Your goal is to develop and inspire team members across the entire workforce. Leaders inspire loyalty when they highlight their team as a strong component within a thriving organization.

Message Peers

Just as your updates need to overview your team's results, you must also prominently recognize support or encouragement from your peers and superiors. This reinforces cooperation, ensures support, and strengthens authority.

Message Achievement

By identifying smaller projects which align with strategic goals, managing them through to completion, and then showcasing them as evidence of the entire organization's advancement and collaboration, you will strengthen employee engagement and respect for management. Management will take notice of your support and afford you an increasing measure of trust and latitude in your activities.

Your communication of your team's accomplishments benefits your direct reports and the staff who report to them. We all like to be recognized for our efforts. Your messaging will encourage other employees to similar exploits and other leaders to follow your example. Celebrating achievements likewise strengthens the authority structure and employee engagement.

Expansion:

14. Authority Takes Responsibility

Lincoln said, "Grant is the first general I have had. You know how it has been with all the rest. As soon as I put a man in command of the Army, he'd come to me with a plan of campaign and about as much as to say, 'Now, I don't believe I can do it, but if you say so, I'll try it on,' and so put the responsibility of success or failure on me. They all wanted me to be the general ... I am glad to find a man that can go ahead without me."[58]

Lincoln and his General Ulysses S. Grant shared similar backgrounds and traits including modesty, pragmatism, and the tenacity to vary tactics until the objective was achieved. Tempered by earlier failures, both men exhibited a strong self-reliance and could quickly assess a situation, wisely use available resources, and take responsibility for the outcome without blaming others.

Lincoln was thrilled to finally have a leader who believed it was his responsibility to wring victories out of the available soldiers and supplies. Grant exercised the authority given him and actually voiced his appreciation for the administration's support to his staff and to the President.[59]

Lincoln and Grant illustrated the conduct and approach leaders need to expand their influence and strengthen their organizations' exercise of authority.

Personal Ownership

What makes some leaders take ownership for solving their areas' problems while others seem never to be responsible? Here are three observations:

Their View of Authority

A client once asked for a way to tell the difference between real managers and those who manage in name only. I replied, "Managers say 'I'll make sure this happens.' Pretenders say, 'I'll try.'"

A leader's willingness to be held personally responsible is a large component of what makes others willing to follow them.

As covered in chapter 3. Authority Delivers Results; managers are positioned within the authority structure to execute and deliver results to benefit the organization. An organization's authority is weakened if even a few managers believe they are only responsible to give orders, and hope for the best.

Their View of Failure

To be fair, some managers could have started with the intention to take personal responsibility for their areas, but initial failures reduced their risk tolerance. In an attempt to avoid political risk they now defer to their superiors on key decisions. Their hope is to shift responsibility back up the chain of command and buy time so others can become involved.

Their objective is to create a safe, accountability-free pocket for themselves within the authority structure. In reality, no such position exists, and even the attempt weakens respect for management. This is exactly what frustrated Lincoln about the Union's generals prior to Grant.

Lincoln and Grant likewise experienced failure but, in contrast, they converted setbacks into learning experiences.

This fear of failure can also cascade into further damage. It can lead some managers to take on more of the burden of leadership and, as a result, trust more in their own efforts and less in their direct reports' abilities. This is the exact opposite of what is required. Lincoln and Grant learned from failures and allowed them to hone their judgment and improve their management.

Their View of Direct Reports

Lincoln and Grant both knew much of their confidence and self-reliance came from their ability to get things done through others—to effectively manage people. The same is true today. Here are a few insights into how they dealt with direct reports:

Selection

- Neither leader easily trusted untested or unknown individuals. They carefully considered before selecting candidates to join their teams.[60] Both realized their leadership potential would be affected by their direct reports' proficiency so they looked for potential leaders with strong and consistent personal character.[61]

Guidance

- Both set the objective before their direct reports, listened to others' opinions to gain insight on the objectives at hand,[62] and then permitted their team members to craft their own plans and tactics.[63] The lack of overly-detailed instructions allowed their staff the freedom and flexibility to exploit opportunities. This increased their teams' commitment to achieving plan details since they developed them. Their approach grew their teams' leadership capability and increased their loyalty, which in turn increased their own leadership influence.

Monitoring

- Neither abandoned their direct reports once objectives were assigned as both continually monitored progress, gave required assistance[64] and occasionally overruled plans.[65] They also knew the importance of being constantly aware of their teams' morale and fighting spirit and would take steps to encourage them when necessary. Lincoln's appreciation of the personal feelings of his army's leadership was apparent the day Grant was promoted to General-in-Chief. Lincoln specifically asked Grant to include in his remarks something which would soothe the feelings of jealousy in the army's most senior officers.[66]

Take Responsibility and Act

General Grant recalled Lincoln's remarks to him the night they finally met at the White House. Lincoln told Grant, "All he wanted or had ever wanted was someone who would take the responsibility and act, and call on him for all of the assistance needed, pledging himself to use all the power of the government in rendering such assistance."[67]

In Grant, Lincoln found a general who took personal responsibility as he, in turn, relied on the talents of his well-selected, well-guided, and ever-monitored officers. Grant knew as his officers and staff became more experienced and confident, they could help him determine the best courses of action and deal with unforeseen obstacles. Lincoln stood by ever-ready, if further aid was required to help his direct reports achieve their objectives.

Faith from Knowledge

In reality, what allows leaders to take personal responsibility is knowing and believing in *themselves*—their courage and ability to think and motivate—and also knowing and believing in their *teams*—what their teams are truly capable of, their potential to rise to meet challenges.

Set your objectives, ask for your team's input, and allow members to plan and execute while overseeing them to ensure progress and inspire enthusiasm. Your ability to take personal responsibility will grow as you develop and demonstrate confidence in your team.

Expansion:

15. Authority Creates Allies

[Lincoln's] "...participation in rough-and-tumble state campaigns had toughened him to criticism, strengthened his belief in democracy, and taught him to rely on his own judgment ... He exhibited an extraordinary patience, which his numerous political failures and difficult marriage surely reinforced, and had learned to control his temper. Long before he became president, he manifested a generous spirit and an unwillingness to nurse political grudges or seek revenge."[68]

In every aspect of his personal, professional, or political life, Lincoln's heartfelt respect and gracious spirit allowed others to more easily support his objectives. Lincoln's own words reveal something of the motivation behind his well-known ability to win over people:

"If you would win a man to your cause, first convince him that you are his sincere friend."[69]

Many can 'turn on' charm for a short period when they sense an opportunity for personal advantage. If disagreements arise or circumstances change, however, those involved, once warmly treated, often experience a rapid cooling.

In contrast, Lincoln was genuinely sincere. Before he was convincing, he was first caring. His consistent integrity and goodwill made people receptive, and this was important to him. He had no time to waste on petty grievances or protracted disagreements.

Lincoln raised this exact subject with his Assistant Secretary of the Navy when the officer seemed to take delight at the prospect of some misfortune coming to a troublesome colleague.

> "You have more of that feeling of personal resentment than I. Perhaps I have too little of it; but I never thought it paid. A man has no time to spend half his life in quarrels. If any man ceases to attack me, I never remember the past against him."[70]

In Lincoln's mind, time needed to provide a return, to advance him toward the accomplishment of his life goal of winning the esteem of others. In addition, his seeking others' esteem led him to value those who could esteem him.

His Life Goal's Affirming Cycle

His choice of personal goal resulted in a self-validating cycle:

- His life goal, to win the esteem of others,
- Caused him to respect those he met,
- Which made them more open to his influence,
- Which increased the potential support available to help him achieve his objectives.

As a result, Lincoln viewed every individual as a prospective source of support, whether they naturally agreed with him or not. For him, it was about treating people honorably and winning support universally from those with whom he related.

Taken from his life's rich storehouse of illustrations, here are a few key principles on how to attract and maintain the support of others.

These are crucial to managers' efforts to build authority and expand influence.

Support from Diverse Opinions

Lincoln believed there was added strength in a variety of opinions and perspectives among those committed to like objectives. Secretary of State William H. Seward echoed Lincoln's belief, saying, "A Cabinet which should agree at once on every such question would be no better or safer than one counselor."[71]

He was self-confident enough to bring strong individuals into his inner circle and make it work; he extended to each a sincere goodwill and then confidently assumed the same goodwill would be returned to him.

Disagreements are inevitable when strong personalities work together, but Lincoln believed in the good nature of those in his Cabinet and held any differences to be of opinion rather than personal at their root.

Once, Lincoln suggested an exchange of some Eastern and Western soldiers to Secretary of War Stanton via a note carried by Congressman Rev. Owen Lovejoy. Their exchange characterizes Lincoln's productive and impersonal attitude.

> "Did Lincoln give you an order of that kind?" "He did, sir," responded Lovejoy. "Then he is a damned fool," thundered Stanton. "Do you mean to say the president is a damned fool?" asked Lovejoy. "Yes, sir, if he gave you such an order as that."
>
> Back in Lincoln's office, Lovejoy recounted his conversation with Stanton. "Did Stanton say I was a damned fool?" Lincoln asked. "He did, sir, and repeated it," said Lovejoy. After a moment's pause, the president looked up and said, "If Stanton said I was a damned fool, then I must be one, for he is nearly always right, and generally says what he means. I will step over and see him."[72]

Lincoln constantly demonstrated his assumption of goodwill among those on his team and was unwilling to let disagreements become personal.

Also note, Lincoln did not send a number of letters ('emails') in an attempt to settle the matter. Written comments are easily misinterpreted since the *tone* of the conversation cannot be effectively nor reliably conveyed. A brief in-person meeting (or video conference call) shows respect, prevents misunderstandings, and saves time.

Support from Opposition

As already mentioned, when challenging others with divergent views, Lincoln worked to see and conceded whatever would be reasonable from their perspectives. To ensure the interchange didn't become personal and depressurize emotions, he frequently admitted his assessment could be incorrect.

> "The lawyer in Lincoln delighted in approaching a question or problem from as many sides as possible, helping him appreciate the views of others, even when those opinions opposed his own."[73]

A newspaper noted this approach in Lincoln's debates, writing, "His language is pure and respectful, he attacks no man's character or motives, but fights with arguments."[74]

Once his respect for the other side was demonstrated by arguing the other side, he laid out his viewpoint and asked individuals for their opinion. The approach heartened opponents and secured results.

Support from Advice

During the last few days of his life, Lincoln, on at least two occasions, abandoned his own position on weighty matters after hearing enthusiastic and well-reasoned arguments from members of his Cabinet.

Lincoln was determined to find the *best* approach for every situation whether or not that approach was purely his or an alloy. His ability to remain teachable to others' opinions was critical in keeping equally talented individuals engaged, as well as ensuring their loyalty and trust.[75]

Release of Negative Comments

Lincoln was humble and magnanimous, willing to ignore 'slights' which would have infuriated and distracted less-secure leaders. By accepting the foibles of others, he remained open to receive their support.

His relationship with Edwin M. Stanton did not start out well but Lincoln's willingness to set aside his own hurt yielded an outstanding Secretary of War and a deep mutual friendship.

Lincoln and Stanton as lawyers were both involved in a case whose interests crossed state boundaries. Each prepared independently but at their first meeting Stanton was thoroughly unkind. After introductions, Stanton gruffly stated to Lincoln and the other lawyers that he would not involve Lincoln because he didn't think they could learn anything from this "long armed ape."[76]

Wounded and shunned by Stanton, Lincoln put away his feelings and watched, now as a spectator, to learn from the presentations of legal arguments. Stanton's logic and reasoning impressed Lincoln but he told his law partner he had been "roughly handled"[77] by Stanton.

Less than seven years later, Lincoln put aside his feelings and asked Stanton to accept the position of Secretary of War, believing his strong personality could aid the effort. It took Stanton a while but he grew to highly respect Lincoln. Lincoln, too, greatly valued Stanton's outstanding service in this vital role and ultimately became close friends with the prickly leader.

The depth of Stanton's personal affection for his Commander in Chief revealed itself as the President lay bleeding from the assassin's bullet. When told by the surgeon Lincoln could not recover, Stanton's associates expected him to stoically issue some directive. Instead, he "burst into loud, convulsive sobs."[78] Lincoln's personal secretary John Hay wrote to Stanton months later.

> "Not every knows, as I do, how close you stood to our lost leader, how he loved you and trusted you, and how vain were all the efforts to shake that trust and confidence, not lightly given & never withdrawn."[79]

Manage Emotions

Passionate leaders often feel opinions deeply and this causes strong emotions to enter into discussions. Lincoln knew how important it was to validate these reactions in both himself and others. Even more critical, he knew one must wait out these sentiments before deciding whether or not their delivery might bring advantage.

Many were blistering rebukes to generals for strategic errors in judgment, such as the letter to General Meade when he failed to follow hard after the Confederate General Lee's army.[80] Others were to his Cabinet members during disagreements such as when he and Seward held different opinions on the resupply of Fort Sumter—which signaled the start of the Civil War—deciding it was better to speak to Seward personally.[81]

This is a vital example for managers due to our ability to instantly send messages and see our words spread across a global social media. Perhaps emotionally-charged communiqués should remain for 24 hours or longer in the 'draft' section of our email programs.

Lincoln "gave the advice that it was healthy to write a hot letter and then burn it."[82] Colonel William H. Crook recalled a smile-provoking example of Lincoln's attempt to instruct Stanton in this method:

> "On one occasion, ... Secretary Stanton was particularly angry with one of the generals ... 'I would like to tell him what I think of him!' he stormed.
>
> "'Why don't you?' Mr. Lincoln agreed. 'Write it all down—do.'

"Mr. Stanton wrote his letter. When it was finished he took it to the President. The President listened to it all.

'All right. Capital!' he nodded. 'And now, Stanton, what are you going to do with it?'

"'Do with it? Why, send it, of course!'

"'I wouldn't,' said the President. 'Throw it in the waste-paper basket.'

"'But it took me two days to write.'

"'Yes, yes, and it did you ever so much good. You feel better now. That is all that is necessary. Just throw it in the basket.'

"After a little more expostulation, into the basket it went."[83]

Extend Mercy

Lincoln remarked to a fellow lawyer, "my impression is that mercy bears richer fruits than any other attribute."[84] The comment again shows the intentionality underlying Lincoln's actions.

Many managers today are short-term in their thinking and too-publicly celebrate when a decision goes their way.

While people have relatively short memories for individual choices as fresh concerns arise, what individuals *do* remember is any negative treatment which may have accompanied a decision. Poor 'sportsmanship' weakens your reputation and embarrasses your direct reports as they continue to work with those from other areas.

In the final days of the Civil War, with victory all but assured, Lincoln surprised his Cabinet colleagues with his grace, whether by asking for 'Dixie,'[85] a favorite song of the Confederates, to be played by a celebrating band, or his exhortation to together "bind up the nation's wounds"[86] in his second inaugural address.

Creating Allies

To create broad support for your objectives, it is best to be sincere and consistent in your efforts and to keep things focused on the *right* decision. Your life goal affects how you view and treat others, which in turn influences their willingness to support you.

Choose to gain support from divergent or opposing viewpoints and the advice of others. Your courage to release past instances of poor treatment will keep you focused on achieving goals rather than settling scores. Validate, but manage your emotions by delaying charged actions and then extend mercy to others, believing you will also receive mercy if ever required.

Leaders who model such an attitude and behaviors will be awarded larger opportunities to guide others.

Expansion:

16. Authority Seeks Opportunity

"Act well your part, there all the honor lies. He who does something at the head of one Regiment, will eclipse him who does nothing at the head of a hundred."[87]

An entitled young general wrote his President a complaining letter which criticized the small scope of his command and accused the War Office of 'punishing' him by assigning him to his current location. Lincoln graciously replied to the self-absorbed leader with universally applicable advice.

Lincoln told the young man, honor—the kind worth seeking—should be found within the quality of a person's own conduct and the manner in which responsibilities are discharged. Lincoln also validated this leader's desire to serve in a larger sphere when he told him the quality of his leadership would be rewarded no matter the size of the command.

Act Well Your Part

Lincoln's admonition to "act well your part," is an effective summary of this book's purpose—to help you succeed as you effectively lead your organization. To lead well and to exercise firm and positive authority over others, your motivation needs to come from within.

Lincoln's life goal, to become worthy of others' esteem, motivated him to act with honor and integrity. Not satisfied with merely matching the behavior of others, he set a high standard for himself, strove to meet it, and then called others to follow his example. This is the definition of leadership.

When you commit yourself to "act well your part" not only will your direct reports and their staff notice but others will too, whether board members or other senior leaders. Don't be unhappy with your current span of control. In patience, believe that your service will be recognized in time. You will soon "eclipse" less disciplined leaders and will be invited to lead larger efforts.

Each fresh area of responsibility expands your campus of higher learning. You will grow administratively, operationally, and personally as you and your team wrestle to set priorities, marshal resources, and direct employees.

While affirming for yourself, the prospect of new areas to lead is critical for your direct reports.

Act for Direct Reports

There are few things more rewarding than accomplishing something of value as a team, where members offset each other's weaknesses and capitalize on collective strengths. Maintaining this 'esprit de corps' is far easier when the group is expanding its influence compared to being static or contracting.

Your ability to take on a new area is directly related to the potential to grow your direct reports' abilities. They should represent a large part of your confidence.

The potential for increased opportunities demonstrates to your direct reports that your area is a place where each must be ready for more.

Opportunities show them why it is valuable to stay and continue to learn with you.

This is also important considering your well-mentored direct reports will be sought after by others within your organization and those outside, as news of your team's accomplishments spreads. While you don't want to hold team members back, you'll want the prospect of expanded responsibilities to make the decision to leave a little more difficult.

If you inspire others, it is likely some of your charges will leave your leadership to test their 'wings.' Take it as a compliment and remain close to mentor them further if at all possible. They will be more likely to support any leadership changes you may make in the future.

Let's leave the discussion of the benefits of new opportunities to present a few proven and practical techniques from our organization's 'toolbox' to improve your chances of rapid success with a new area:

Before Accepting a New Area

Underlying Issues

Watch for an area which may have 'used up' several leaders before it was offered to you. As discussed in "Authority Evaluates Performance," don't quickly assume ineffectual individuals are the cause of an area's deficiency. Watch for underlying systems, incentives, and rewards exerting pressure on decision-making. Your plan needs to include the time and energy to correct these contradictory policies, goals, performance targets, and/or incentives and align them to the 'new' direction you want to pursue.

Consider Suggesting an 'Acting' Role

If senior management offers you a perennial problem area or an area which may stretch you beyond your limits, you may briefly consider suggesting that they let you manage the area in an 'acting role'. Here are some points to consider:

- You don't want a failure, but fear isn't your issue. It may be more the configuration of the area and your ability to rapidly reform whatever opposing expectations currently make the area difficult to manage. You are looking for time to improve the area's structures prior to committing 100%.

- Be aware of *who* may be behind the opposing expectations driving the area. Powerful sponsors may need more time to adjust their approach regarding a 'pet' project or area.

- In some cases, an 'acting' role can give your observations a higher degree of objectivity as you evaluate the new area and its expectations.

- Depending on your organization's culture, however, even the suggestion of an 'acting role' may be interpreted as a lack of confidence rather than a testing period to see what can be done prior to launching out from your existing role.

Consider this option, but decide quickly to reinforce your reputation as a decisive leader.

After Accepting Your New Area

Go to School

Once you're leading the new area, work to be a 'quick study' without jumping too quickly to conclusions. Research the situation and listen to all sides until you have sufficient information to proceed.

"When Lincoln became President he knew little about military strategy and tactics. He worked swiftly to correct this deficiency. He listened, consulted, questioned, and challenged those more skilled until his natural instincts and abilities integrated his new-found knowledge. At the end of the Civil War Lincoln's ability as a strategist-tactician was widely recognized."[88]

Honor their Past

After you've finished preliminary plans for the new area, meet with those involved, but first study the area's history, however short, within the organization. Identify positive examples where they successfully adapted to previous changes and how their actions contributed positively to today's enterprise. Encapsulate the findings into a brief presentation to insert at the beginning of your meetings. These few minutes pay rich dividends.

People are more willing to hear about *your* 'new' future once *their* past accomplishments are affirmed. Tell them their previously exhibited passion is exactly what is needed to successfully navigate upcoming events. The fact that you took the time to research their contributions will help them to view you as a leader they can trust going forward.

Affirm their Present

When learning a new area, listen to those involved and avoid giving them the impression that 'everything is broken but we're here to help.' Educating leaders with firmly-held, preconceived notions is frustrating for those trying to educate them and counter-productive for the leaders, as people soon give up trying to reorient them and stop offering valuable advice.

As a general rule, the regular activities within an area evolve over time in response to external and internal demands, as no-longer-needed activities drop off and newly required activities are added.

Therefore, unless you radically change a group's mandate, the *new* activity set will look surprisingly similar to the *old* activity set. Recognizing this, approach personnel to listen for what is good and affirm it, then look for what is not optimal and identify the causes of these exceptions.

Present the Rationale

When there is a 'business case,' which describes the rationale for imminent changes, you should summarize and present it in your meetings. This will be well received, especially in the organization's operational divisions. Most often when these areas face change, personnel are told *what* they must do differently, as opposed to *why* they need to do things differently.

The flawed assumption is that those in these areas don't care or wouldn't fully understand. Sharing a summarized version of the 'business case' is a sign you respect the intellects of valued employees, who, now armed with a broader viewpoint, can help their leaders avoid costly and embarrassing missteps.

Just as 'honoring their past' frees *hearts* to follow, 'presenting the rationale' frees *heads* to unequivocally follow.

Present Half-Finished Ideas

The objective of any change in activity is for the people involved to 'own' the changes, to apply their deep experience to the prospective changes, and to see things to a successful outcome. Nothing is more effective in this regard than presenting half-finished ideas and letting groups 'roll up their sleeves' and complete the planning and execution.

> Working with one particular client, I had an idea which had the potential to reduce delivery time knowing such an acceleration would give the company an immediate and substantial marketing advantage.
>
> On a Friday afternoon, I brought the department heads together and in fifteen minutes explained the opportunity, my preliminary

idea to cut delivery in half, and asked each to give me their reactions to the idea.

I spent the next 90 minutes hearing the question, "Have you thought of...?" I endlessly replied, "No, I haven't thought of anything other than what I explained to you and wanted you to consider. I can't say if this will work, but if anyone can, I know the people in this room have the knowledge and experience to find a way, if it makes sense."

On Monday afternoon, each of them found me and said, "I've been thinking about this all weekend. I've got ideas that can really help us."

They presented to senior management their composite plan, much better than any I envisioned, and charged ahead. Delivery times dropped by half, sales increased sharply, and the owners accepted a purchase offer for the company from a multi-national. These achievements were in large part due to the operational and marketplace success sparked by a team who took a half-finished idea and made it their own.

Share Uncertainty

"Lincoln's willingness to openly discuss his doubts is a distinguishing characteristic of his political leadership."[89]

There is a beguiling aspect, both informational and emotional, in Lincoln's willingness to admit that he may be mistaken, even in the midst of attempts to win a group to his viewpoint.

Lincoln's admission left his listeners more willing to express supporting or opposing viewpoints. Lincoln gained a deeper insight from any new information which allowed him to make adjustments and become even more convincing.

Lincoln's admission communicated a humility and an openness to others' opinions which caused a corresponding increase in goodwill. In addition, potential opponents saw little to gain from fighting with a person who had already admitted he could be wrong. Lincoln's approach defused disagreements before they could form.

Share Confidence

One of your most important jobs as a leader is to make sure your direct reports know how much you appreciate them. Your direct reports represent your leadership capability to a great degree, as previously mentioned, and you'll want to monitor their morale, enthusiasm and engagement. Make time to periodically sit down (if at all possible) with each one to let them know how you think they are doing. This is in addition to your annual review.

You also need to make sure they know how much you value their contribution and leadership. Look for unique ways to recognize over-and-above examples of courage, innovation, or leadership. Read your culture and discover what might motivate your team's members. Don't over-recognize, as that reduces the significance of your appreciation. Consider for each person what might be a significant stretch in capabilities and watch for notable examples.

This type of recognition has nothing whatsoever to do with budget. One mentor motivated his team with small notes containing only the words "Good Job" and the manager's initials. The worth of these tiny notes was based on the laws of supply and demand. Every year only approximately 20 were distributed and only for significant efforts. If a person received a few, they considered themselves appreciated.

Let them know your confidence as a leader is based on their talent, creativity, and commitment to follow things through to completion.

Natural Outflow

Your demonstration of authority-building leadership will undoubtedly attract growth opportunities—if not within your organization, then in others. Take these offers as recognition of your ability to coordinate and your team's ability to deliver.

Consider each opportunity and negotiate acceptable terms of support and time allowed for the transition. Once decided, get your team involved in establishing what must be done and use the opportunity to grow their individual capabilities. Be sincere and encouraging in your guidance and direction, and prepare to be amazed by their accomplishments.

Summary

The Lincoln Authority describes a model of the core responsibility of leadership: the management of others for collective benefit. In many ways it is a lofty standard, both for its particular power when deployed and for the personal challenge leaders will face as they attempt to align themselves against its tenants.

We all miss the mark on occasion. Our natural reactions can at times be difficult to moderate. But when you and your colleagues begin to apply the principles contained in *The Lincoln Authority* in your daily interactions, the difference will be noticeable within your teams and across your organizations.

The goal of a model is not perfect conformity but rather progressive competency—to increase our proficiency over time.

In one speech, Lincoln also referred to a lofty model of human behavior. He said "... let it be as nearly reached as we can."[90] It is my sincere wish that your expression of leadership reflect an increasing likeness to the model articulated within *The Lincoln Authority* and the standard set by Lincoln himself.

Expansion:

17. Next Steps

Here are some practical suggestions for you to broaden the impact of the principles contained in *The Lincoln Authority*:

For Individuals:

To help you continue to grow in your respect of and service to others:

- Set a life goal similar to the one Lincoln set for himself, to earn the esteem of others.
- Find a cause to help others, especially one which cannot come back and benefit you.

To help you apply the concepts in your daily leadership:

- Find a peer leader within your organization, read the chapters one at a time, and then get together over lunch or a coffee (or some alternative) to discuss and suggest ways to apply the concepts. This book provides a common leadership vocabulary you can use with each other.
- In a similar fashion, you could also suggest *The Lincoln Authority* to your immediate manager to go through one chapter a

month in your management meetings. This might be an excellent way to educate your peers and help the entire organization.

To help other leaders:

- Suggest they also read the book or send them a copy as a gift.

For Your Direct Reports:

- Tell them your plan to review and discuss one chapter at a time in your monthly management meeting. Appoint a rotating schedule of direct reports to summarize the chapter's main points to kick off the discussion, to ensure people read prior to coming. This is a great way to learn practical content together and to keep each other accountable to make adjustments and improvements. Again, this book provides you all with a common leadership vocabulary to encourage, caution, and advise each other.

- Look for *The Lincoln Authority* Study Guide to be released. Check *thelincolnauthority.com* for release and purchase information.

- If your direct reports have their own teams, ask them to consider the monthly meeting discussion. The operational and financial benefits of higher levels of employee engagement should help you decide.

For Your Organization:

- Suggest *The Lincoln Authority* to the leaders of your Human Resources, Learning Center, or Center of Excellence. You could provide a copy to them as a show of support (at the risk of appearing overly self-serving). These leaders are always looking for practical content to improve business performance so they will appreciate your gesture.

- As a senior leader, you may want to list *The Lincoln Authority* as a recommended resource on your LinkedIn or internal corporate profile.

- Link to the book in one of your newsletter articles or updates to your leadership team.

- *The Lincoln Authority* could be included as a focus of your organization's annual leadership meeting. Leaders could share how the book influenced their practice of leadership in the previous year. As a practical guidebook to help managers exercise authority with more power and consideration, it could trigger a revival of purpose and respect for others.

- Contact the author to speak or conduct a workshop or breakout session at a corporate leadership conference.

Feedback

- Go to *amazon.com* and/or *thelincolnauthority.com* and leave your review or feedback on how this book has shaped your exercise of authority.

- For suggestions on future content or other constructive criticism, please leave such comments on *thelincolnauthority.com*.

Notes:

Notes:

Notes:

Notes:

Endnotes

1 Stakelberg, Count S., "Tolstoi Holds Lincoln World's Greatest Hero", *The Library of America - Story of the Week*, link: http://www.loa.org/images/pdf/Tolstoy_on_Lincoln.pdf, Reprinted from "The Lincoln Anthology: Great Writers on His Life and Legacy from 1860 to Now," *The Library of America*, 2009, 387–388. © Copyright 2009 Literary Classics of the U.S., Inc. First appeared in the February 7, 1909, issue of the New York World.

2 http://www.gallup.com/strategicconsulting/163007/state-american-workplace.aspx

3 Foner, Eric (2011-09-26), *The Fiery Trial: Abraham Lincoln and American Slavery*, W. W. Norton & Company, Kindle Edition, Location 209.

4 Richard H. Abbott, *Cobbler in Congress: The Life of Henry Wilson, 1812–1875*, The University Press of Kentucky, July 1982, 156; as quoted in "Abraham Lincoln's Personality," in *Abraham Lincoln's Classroom* by the Lehrman Institute and the Lincoln Institute link: http://abrahamlincolnsclassroom.org/abraham-lincoln-in-depth/abraham-lincolns-personality/

5 http://www.gallup.com/strategicconsulting/163007/state-american-workplace.aspx

6 Gienapp, William E. (2002-04-08), *Abraham Lincoln and Civil War America: A Biography*, Oxford University Press, Kindle Edition, Locations 2342–2344.

7 Mulder, Raymond J., personal communication

8 White Jr., Ronald C. (2009-01-06), *A. Lincoln: A Biography*, Random House Publishing Group, Kindle Edition, Location 10144.

9 Keegan, John, "A Brit Rates Our Generals," *Civil War Times*, December 2009, 58,

as quoted in, "Abraham Lincoln as Commander-in-Chief" in *Abraham Lincoln's Classroom*, by the Lehrman Institute and the Lincoln Institute, link: http://abrahamlincolnsclassroom.org/abraham-lincoln-in-depth/abraham-lincoln-as-commander-in-chief/

[10] Mulder, Raymond J., personal communication

[11] Wilson, Douglas L., ed.; Davis, Rodney O., ed.; Sweet, Leonard. 'Leonard Swett to William H. Herndon' in *Herndon's Informants: Letters, Interviews, and Statements About Abraham Lincoln*, University of Illinois Press, 1998. [format: book], [genre: letter]. Permission: University of Illinois Press, Persistent link: http://lincoln.lib.niu.edu/file.php?file=herndon162.html

[12] Rufus Rockwell Wilson, editor, *Intimate Memories of Lincoln*, (George Hartley, Chicago News), 1909, 600; as quoted in "Employees and Staff: Edward Duffield Neill (1823–1893)" in *Mr. Lincoln's Whitehouse*, by the Lehrman Institute and the Lincoln Institute, link: http://www.mrlincolnswhitehouse.org/inside.asp?ID=62&subjectID=2.

[13] Mulder, Raymond J., pers. comm.

[14] Mulder, Raymond J., pers. comm.

[15] Michael Burlingame and John R. Turner Ettlinger, editors, *Inside Lincoln's White House: The Complete Civil War Diary of John Hay (September 25, 1864)*, 232; as quoted in "Abraham Lincoln and George B. McClellan," in *Abraham Lincoln's Classroom* by the Lehrman Institute and the Lincoln Institute, link: http://abrahamlincolnsclassroom.org/abraham-lincolns-contemporaries/abraham-lincoln-and-george-b-mcclellan/

[16] Mulder, Raymond J., pers. comm.

[17] Burlingame, Michael, "Letter from John Hay to John G. Nicolay, August 10, 1885; Nicolay and Hay: Court Historians", *Journal of the Abraham Lincoln Association*, Winter 1998, 3; as quoted in "Abraham Lincoln and George B. McClellan," in *Abraham Lincoln's Classroom* by the Lehrman Institute and the Lincoln Institute, link: http://abrahamlincolnsclassroom.org/abraham-lincolns-contemporaries/abraham-lincoln-and-george-b-mcclellan/

[18] "Abraham Lincoln to George B. McClellan, November 5, 1862," *Collected Works of Abraham Lincoln*, Vol. V, 485; as quoted by White Jr., Ronald C. (2009-01-06), *A. Lincoln: A Biography*, Random House Publishing Group, Kindle Edition, Locations 9685–9686.

[19] Letter from George B. McClellan to Mary Ellen McClellan, July 27, 1861, *The Civil War Papers of George B. McClellan: Selected Correspondence, 1860–1865*, Stephen W. Sears, editor, 70; as quoted in "Abraham Lincoln and George B. McClellan," in *Abraham Lincoln's Classroom* by the Lehrman Institute and the Lincoln Institute, link: http://abrahamlincolnsclassroom.org/abraham-lincolns-contemporaries/abraham-lincoln-and-george-b-mcclellan/

[20] Mulder, Raymond J., pers. comm.

[21] Henry Clay Whitney, *Life on the Circuit with Lincoln*, Estes and Lauriat, 1892, 119; as quoted in "Abraham Lincoln's Personality," in *Abraham Lincoln's Classroom* by the Lehrman Institute and the Lincoln Institute, link: http://abrahamlincolnsclassroom.org/abraham-lincoln-in-depth/abraham-lincolns-personality/

[22] Kunhardt, Philip B. III, "Lincoln's Contested Legacy," *Smithsonian Magazine*, February 2009, link: http://www.smithsonianmag.com/history/lincolns-contested-legacy-44978351/?all

[23] Barton, William E., *President Lincoln*, The Bobbs-Merrill Company, 1933, 63–64; as quoted by White Jr., Ronald C. (2009-01-06), *A. Lincoln: A Biography*, Random House Publishing Group, Kindle Edition, Location 5761–5786.

[24] Abraham Lincoln, "Reply to Pennsylvania Delegation," March 5, 1861, *Collected Works of Abraham Lincoln*, Vol. 4, 274, by The Lincoln Association, University of Michigan Digital Text Collections, link: http://quod.lib.umich.edu/l/lincoln/lincoln4/1:394?rgn=div1;view=full text

[25] "Remarks at the Funeral Services held in Concord, April 19, 1865," *The Complete Works of Ralph Waldo Emerson*, Volume XI; as quoted in "Abraham Lincoln's Personality" in *Abraham Lincoln's Classroom* by the Lehrman Institute and the Lincoln Institute, link: http://abrahamlincolnsclassroom.org/abraham-lincoln-in-depth/abraham-lincolns-personality

[26] Burlingame, Michael, *The Inner World of Abraham Lincoln*, University of Illinois Press, 1997, 8.

[27] Lincoln, Abraham, "Speech to the Springfield Washington Temperance Society", February 22, 1842, *Collected Works of Abraham*

Lincoln, Vol. 1, 271–279, University of Michigan Digital Text Collections, link: http://quod.lib.umich.edu/l/lincoln/lincoln1/1:294?rgn=div1;view=fulltext

[28] Gienapp, William E. (2002-04-08), *Abraham Lincoln and Civil War America: A Biography*, Oxford University Press, Kindle Edition, Locations 370–372.

[29] Winkler, H. Donald, "The Women in Lincoln's Life," in Thomas, Benjamin P., *Lincoln's New Salem*, Southern Illinois University Press, Revised Edition, 1988, 53; as quoted in "Abraham Lincoln's Personality," in *Abraham Lincoln's Classroom* by the Lehrman Institute and the Lincoln Institute, link: http://abrahamlincolnsclassroom.org/abraham-lincoln-in-depth/abraham-lincolns-personality/

[30] Burlingame, Michael, ed., "Robert Todd Lincoln interviewed by John G. Nicolay, 5 January 1885", in *An Oral History of Abraham Lincoln: John G. Nicolay's Interviews and Essays*, Southern Illinois University Press, 1996, 88–89; as quoted in *John Hopkins University Blog*, July 3 2013, link: http://jhupressblog.com/2013/07/03/on-whether-lincoln-ordered-an-attack-on-the-retreating-lee/

[31] Gideon Welles, *"Diary of Gideon Welles,"* Vol. 1, 23–25; as quoted in "Cabinet and Vice Presidents: William H. Seward (1801–1872)" in *Mr. Lincoln's Whitehouse* by the Lehrman Institute and the Lincoln Institute, link: http://www.mrlincolnswhitehouse.org/inside.asp?ID=93&subjectID=2

[32] White Jr., Ronald C. (2009-01-06), *A. Lincoln: A Biography*, Random House Publishing Group, Kindle Edition, Locations 6025–6027.

[33] White Jr., Ronald C. (2009-01-06), *A. Lincoln: A Biography*, Random House Publishing Group, Kindle Edition, Locations 10473–10475.

[34] Fraker, Guy C., *Lincoln's Ladder to the Presidency: The Eighth Judicial Circuit*, SIU Press, November 9, 2012, 62.

[35] White Jr., Ronald C. (2009-01-06), *A. Lincoln: A Biography*, Random House Publishing Group, Kindle Edition, Location 8587.

[36] "Augustus K. Riggin interview with William H. Herndon, March 7, 1887," Douglas L. Wilson and Rodney O. Davis, editors, *Herndon's*

Informants: Letters, Interviews, and Statements about Abraham Lincoln, University of Illinois Press, 1998, 603; as quoted in "Abraham Lincoln's Personality," in *Abraham Lincoln's Classroom* by the Lehrman Institute and the Lincoln Institute; link: http://abrahamlincolnsclassroom.org/abraham-lincoln-in-depth/abraham-lincolns-personality/

37 Benjamin Thomas, "Abe Lincoln, Country Lawyer", *The Atlantic*, February 1954; as quoted in "Abraham Lincoln's Personality," in *Abraham Lincoln's Classroom* by the Lehrman Institute and the Lincoln Institute; link: http://abrahamlincolnsclassroom.org/abraham-lincoln-in-depth/abraham-lincolns-personality/

38 Jack Welch, Interview with Dr. Henry Cloud on Leadership, Leadercast 2013, Giant Impact, personal communication.

39 Miles, Keith N., *The Improvement Toolbox*, Streamlined Press 1997, 60.

40 Helen Nicolay, "Lincoln's Cabinet", *The Abraham Lincoln Quarterly*, March 1949, 275–276; as quoted in "Abraham Lincoln's Personality," in *Abraham Lincoln's Classroom* by the Lehrman Institute and the Lincoln Institute; link: http://abrahamlincolnsclassroom.org/abraham-lincoln-in-depth/abraham-lincolns-personality/

41 Owens, Mackubin T., "Commander-in-Chief," *Claremont Review of Books*, Winter 2008–2009, 60; as quoted in "Abraham Lincoln as Commander in Chief," in *Abraham Lincoln's Classroom* by the Lehrman Institute and the Lincoln Institute; link: http://abrahamlincolnsclassroom.org/abraham-lincoln-in-depth/abraham-lincoln-as-commander-in-chief/

42 Gienapp, William E. (2002-04-08), *Abraham Lincoln and Civil War America: A Biography*, Oxford University Press, Kindle Edition, Location 2180.

43 Mulder, Raymond J., pers. comm.

44 Burlingame, Michael, *Abraham Lincoln: A Life*, Vol. II, Johns Hopkins University Press, 2008, 426; as quoted in "Abraham Lincoln as Commander in Chief" in *Abraham Lincoln's Classroom* by the Lehrman Institute and the Lincoln Institute; link: http://abrahamlincolnsclassroom.org/abraham-lincoln-in-depth/abraham-lincoln-as-commander-in-chief/

[45] "Letter from George B. McClellan to Mary Ellen McClellan, July 27, 1861", Stephen W. Sears, editor, *The Civil War Papers of George B. McClellan: Selected Correspondence, 1860–1865*, 70; as quoted in "Abraham Lincoln and George B. McClellan," within *Abraham Lincoln's Classroom* by the Lehrman Institute and the Lincoln Institute; link: http://abrahamlincolnsclassroom.org/abraham-lincolns-contemporaries/abraham-lincoln-and-george-b-mcclellan/

[46] http://en.wikipedia.org/wiki/Lee_Ross

[47] Miles, Keith N., *The Improvement Toolbox*, Streamlined Press, 1997, 109.

[48] Symonds, Craig L., "Lincoln and His Admirals," John Y. Simon, Harold Holzer, and Dawn Vogel, editors, *Lincoln Revisited*, 213; as quoted in "Abraham Lincoln as Commander in Chief," in *Abraham Lincoln's Classroom* by the Lehrman Institute and the Lincoln Institute; link: http://abrahamlincolnsclassroom.org/abraham-lincoln-in-depth/abraham-lincoln-as-commander-in-chief/

[49] Chittenden, Lucius E., *Recollections of President Lincoln and His Administration*, 423; as quoted in "The War Effort: Fort Stevens," in *Mr. Lincoln's White House* by the Lincoln Institute and the Lehrman Institute; link: http://www.mrlincolnswhitehouse.org/www_redesign/inside.asp?ID=127&subjectID=4

[50] "Conversation with Lafayette Foster, October 23, 1878," Michael Burlingame, editor, *An Oral History of Abraham Lincoln, John G. Nicolay's Interviews and Essays*, 53; as quoted in "Abraham Lincoln and Salmon P. Chase," in *Abraham Lincoln's Classroom* by the Lincoln Institute and the Lehrman Institute, link: http://abrahamlincolnsclassroom.org/abraham-lincolns-contemporaries/abraham-lincoln-and-salmon-p-chase/

[51] Gideon Welles, *Diary of Gideon Welles*, Houghton Mifflin, 1911, Vol. II, 158; as quoted in "Abraham Lincoln and Salmon P. Chase," in *Abraham Lincoln's Classroom* by the Lincoln Institute and the Lehrman Institute; link: http://abrahamlincolnsclassroom.org/abraham-lincolns-contemporaries/abraham-lincoln-and-salmon-p-chase/

[52] Simon, John Y., "Lincoln and Halleck," Charles Hubbard, editor, *Lincoln and His Contemporaries*, 83; as quoted in "Abraham Lincoln as Commander in Chief," in *Abraham Lincoln's Classroom* by the Lehrman

Institute and the Lincoln Institute; link:
http://abrahamlincolnsclassroom.org/abraham-lincoln-in-depth/abraham-lincoln-as-commander-in-chief/

53 Symonds, Craig L., *Lincoln and His Admirals*, Oxford University Press, 2010, 290; as quoted in "Abraham Lincoln as Commander in Chief," in *Abraham Lincoln's Classroom* by the Lehrman Institute and the Lincoln Institute; link:
http://abrahamlincolnsclassroom.org/abraham-lincoln-in-depth/abraham-lincoln-as-commander-in-chief/

54 Abraham Lincoln, "Notes for Speeches," August 21, 1858, *Collected Works of Abraham Lincoln*, Vol. 2, 553, by The Lincoln Association, University of Michigan Digital Text Collections, link:
http://quod.lib.umich.edu/l/lincoln/lincoln2/1:568?rgn=div1;view=fulltext

55 Barton, William E., *The Life of Abraham Lincoln*, Books Inc., Vol. I, 409; as quoted in "Historian's Comments—Cooper Union Speech," in *Mr. Lincoln and New York* by the Lincoln Institute, link:
http://www.mrlincolnandnewyork.org/inside.asp?ID=18&subjectID=2

56 Hubbard, Charles M., *Lincoln Reshapes the Presidency* (Phillip Shaw Paludan, "Lincoln and the Greeley Letter: An Exposition"), 83; as quoted in "Abraham Lincoln and Emancipation," in *Abraham Lincoln's Classroom* by the Lehrman Institute and the Lincoln Institute, link:
http://abrahamlincolnsclassroom.org/abraham-lincoln-in-depth/abraham-lincoln-and-emancipation/

57 Coutu, Diane, "Leadership Lessons from Abraham Lincoln—A Conversation with Historian Doris Kearns Goodwin", *Harvard Business Review*, February 2009, PDF, 3, Copyright © 2009 Harvard Business School Publishing Corporation. All Rights Reserved

58 Burlingame, Michael, *Abraham Lincoln: A Life*, Johns Hopkins University Press, 2008, Vol. II, 655; as quoted in "Abraham Lincoln as Commander in Chief," in website *Abraham Lincoln's Classroom* by the Lehrman Institute and the Lincoln Institute; link:
http://abrahamlincolnsclassroom.org/abraham-lincoln-in-depth/abraham-lincoln-as-commander-in-chief/

59 "Letter from Ulysses S. Grant to Abraham Lincoln, May 1, 1864," *Abraham Lincoln Papers at the Library of Congress*, Transcribed and Annotated by the Lincoln Studies Center, Knox College. Galesburg,

Illinois; as quoted in "Abraham Lincoln and Ulysses S. Grant," in *Abraham Lincoln's Classroom* by the Lehrman Institute and the Lincoln Institute; link: http://abrahamlincolnsclassroom.org/abraham-lincolns-contemporaries/abraham-lincoln-and-ulysses-s-grant/

⁶⁰ Goss, Thomas J., *The War Within the Union High Command*, University Press of Kansas, 191; Jones, R. Steven, *The Right Hand of Command: Use & Disuse of Personal Staffs in the Civil War*, Stackpole Books, May 1, 2000, 191; as quoted in "Abraham Lincoln and Ulysses S. Grant," in *Abraham Lincoln's Classroom* by the Lehrman Institute and the Lincoln Institute; link: http://abrahamlincolnsclassroom.org/abraham-lincolns-contemporaries/abraham-lincoln-and-ulysses-s-grant/

⁶¹ Eaton, John, *Grant, Lincoln and the Freedmen: Reminiscences of the Civil War*, Longmans, Green, and Company, 1907, 88; as quoted in "Abraham Lincoln and Ulysses S. Grant," in *Abraham Lincoln's Classroom* by the Lehrman Institute and the Lincoln Institute; link: http://abrahamlincolnsclassroom.org/abraham-lincolns-contemporaries/abraham-lincoln-and-ulysses-s-grant/

⁶² Symonds, Craig L., "Lincoln and His Admirals," John Y. Simon, Harold Holzer, and Dawn Vogel, editors, *Lincoln Revisited*, 212; as quoted in "Abraham Lincoln as Commander-in-Chief," in *Abraham Lincoln's Classroom* by the Lehrman Institute and the Lincoln Institute; link: http://abrahamlincolnsclassroom.org/abraham-lincoln-in-depth/abraham-lincoln-as-commander-in-chief/

⁶³ Smith, Jean Edward, *Ulysses S. Grant*, Simon & Schuster, 2000, 202; as quoted in "Abraham Lincoln and Ulysses S. Grant," in *Abraham Lincoln's Classroom* by the Lehrman Institute and the Lincoln Institute; link: http://abrahamlincolnsclassroom.org/abraham-lincolns-contemporaries/abraham-lincoln-and-ulysses-s-grant/

⁶⁴ Maurice, Frederick, *Soldiers and Statesmen*, Little, Brown, and Company, 1926, 105; as quoted in "Abraham Lincoln and Ulysses S. Grant," in *Abraham Lincoln's Classroom* by the Lehrman Institute and the Lincoln Institute; link: http://abrahamlincolnsclassroom.org/abraham-lincolns-contemporaries/abraham-lincoln-and-ulysses-s-grant/

⁶⁵ Current, Richard N., *The Lincoln Nobody Knows*, Farrar, Straus and Giroux, 1958, 159–160; as quoted in "Abraham Lincoln and Ulysses S. Grant," in *Abraham Lincoln's Classroom* by the Lehrman Institute and

the Lincoln Institute; link:
http://abrahamlincolnsclassroom.org/abraham-lincolns-contemporaries/abraham-lincoln-and-ulysses-s-grant/

66 Burlingame, Michael, *Abraham Lincoln: A Life*, Johns Hopkins University Press, 2008, Vol. II, 110; as quoted in "Abraham Lincoln as Commander-in-Chief," in *Abraham Lincoln's Classroom* by the Lehrman Institute and the Lincoln Institute; link:
http://abrahamlincolnsclassroom.org/abraham-lincoln-in-depth/abraham-lincoln-as-commander-in-chief/

67 Ulysses S. Grant, *Personal Memoirs of Ulysses S. Grant*, Charles L. Webster & Company, 1885, Vol. II, 122; as quoted in "Abraham Lincoln and Ulysses S. Grant," in *Abraham Lincoln's Classroom* by the Lehrman Institute and the Lincoln Institute; link:
http://abrahamlincolnsclassroom.org/abraham-lincolns-contemporaries/abraham-lincoln-and-ulysses-s-grant/

68 Gienapp, William E. (2002-04-08), *Abraham Lincoln and Civil War America: A Biography*, Oxford University Press, Kindle Edition, Locations 3256–3260.

69Lincoln, Abraham, "Address to Springfield Washington Temperance Society", February 22d, 1842, *Collected Works of Abraham Lincoln*, Vol. 1, 273, by The Lincoln Association, University of Michigan General Digital Collection, link:
http://quod.lib.umich.edu/l/lincoln/lincoln1/1:294?rgn=div1;view=fulltext

70 Schott, Thomas E., "Letter from Alexander Stephens to Linton Stephens, October 13, 1854," *Alexander H. Stephens of Georgia: A Biography*, Louisiana State University Press, 1996, 176; as quoted in "Abraham Lincoln and Alexander H. Stephens," in the *Abraham Lincoln's Classroom* by the Lehrman Institute and the Lincoln Institute; link: http://abrahamlincolnsclassroom.org/abraham-lincolns-contemporaries/abraham-lincoln-and-alexander-h-stephens/

71 Seward, William Henry, *The Diplomatic History of the War for the Union*, Houghton, Mifflin, 1883, 527.

72 Shirley, Ralph, *A Short Life of Abraham Lincoln*, Funk & Wagnalls, 1919, Forgotten Books, 2013, 112–113, link:
http://www.forgottenbooks.org/readbook_text/A_Short_Life_of_Abraham_Lincoln_1000445291/123

[73] White Jr., Ronald C. (2009-01-06), *A. Lincoln: A Biography*, Random House Publishing Group, Kindle Edition, Locations 231–232.

[74] White Jr., Ronald C. (2009-01-06), *A. Lincoln: A Biography*, Random House Publishing Group, Kindle Edition, Locations 4315–4316.

[75] Goodwin, Doris Kearns (2006-12-08), *Team of Rivals: The Political Genius of Abraham Lincoln*, Simon & Schuster, Kindle Edition, Locations 14943–14944 and 14974–14977.

[76] Gienapp, William E. (2002-04-08), *Abraham Lincoln and Civil War America: A Biography*, Oxford University Press, Kindle Edition, Locations 855–859.

[77] Kauffman, Michael W., *American Brutus: John Wilkes Booth and the Lincoln Conspiracies*, Random House Publishing Group, 2005, 34; as quoted in "Abraham Lincoln and Edwin Stanton" in the *Abraham Lincoln's Classroom* by the Lehrman Institute and the Lincoln Institute; link: http://abrahamlincolnsclassroom.org/abraham-lincolns-contemporaries/abraham-lincoln-and-edwin-stanton/

[78] Kauffman, Michael W. (2007-12-18), *American Brutus: John Wilkes Booth and the Lincoln Conspiracies*, Random House Publishing Group, Kindle Edition, Location 769–770.

[79] Burlingame, Michael, *Abraham Lincoln: The Observations of John G. Nicolay and John Hay*, South Illinois University Press, 2007, 89; as quoted in "Abraham Lincoln and Edwin Stanton" in the *Abraham Lincoln's Classroom* by the Lehrman Institute and the Lincoln Institute; link: http://abrahamlincolnsclassroom.org/abraham-lincolns-contemporaries/abraham-lincoln-and-edwin-stanton/

[80] "Abraham Lincoln to George G. Meade, Tuesday, July 14, 1863," Scanned letter, Library of Congress, *The Abraham Lincoln Papers at the Library of Congress*, Link: http://memory.loc.gov/cgi-bin/ampage?collId=mal&fileName=mal1/248/2480600/malpage.db&recNum=0

[81] White Jr., Ronald C. (2009-01-06), *A. Lincoln: A Biography*, Random House Publishing Group, Kindle Edition, Locations 7550–7551.

[82] Sandburg, Carl, *Abraham Lincoln; The Prairie Years*, Harcourt, Brace, and Company Inc., 1926, 301, University of Michigan General Digital Collection, link:

http://quod.lib.umich.edu/g/genpub/ACK7971.0002.001?rgn=main;vie
w=fulltext

83 Crook, William H., *Through Five Administrations: Reminiscences of
Colonel William H. Crook*, Margarita Spalding Gerry, Editor, Kessinger
Publishing, 2008, 34; as quoted in "Abraham Lincoln's Personality," in
Abraham Lincoln's Classroom by the Lehrman Institute and the Lincoln
Institute link: http://abrahamlincolnsclassroom.org/abraham-lincoln-
in-depth/abraham-lincolns-personality/

84 Belz, Herman, "Lincoln's View of Direct Democracy and Public
Opinion," Elliott Abrams, Editor, *Democracy—how Direct?: Views from
the Founding Era and the Polling Era*, 34; as quoted on, "Abraham
Lincoln's Values and Philosophy," in *Abraham Lincoln's Classroom* by
the Lehrman Institute and the Lincoln Institute, link:
http://abrahamlincolnsclassroom.org/abraham-lincoln-in-
depth/abraham-lincolns-values-and-philosophy/

85 Gienapp, William E. (2002-04-08), *Abraham Lincoln and Civil War
America: A Biography*, Oxford University Press, Kindle Edition,
Locations 3366–3367.

86 Lincoln, Abraham (2013-04-13). *The Writings of Abraham Lincoln:
All Volumes*, Waxkeep Publishing, Kindle Edition, Locations 24984–
24985.

87 "Letter from Abraham Lincoln to David Hunter, December 31, 1861,
Collected Works of Abraham Lincoln, Vol. V, 85, University of Michigan
General Digital Collection, link:
http://quod.lib.umich.edu/l/lincoln/lincoln5/1:181?rgn=div1;view=fullt
ext

88 McPherson, James M., "Lincoln as Commander-in-Chief",
Smithsonian Magazine, January 2009, link:
http://www.smithsonianmag.com/history/lincoln-as-commander-in-
chief-131322819/#ixzz2v7MNmqPm

89 White Jr., Ronald C. (2009-01-06), *A. Lincoln: A Biography*, Random
House Publishing Group, Kindle Edition, Locations 11506–11507.

90 Lincoln, Abraham, "Speech at Chicago, Illinois, July 10, 1858,"
Collected Works of Abraham Lincoln, Roy P. Basler, Editor, Volume II,
501; University of Michigan General Digital Collection, link:

http://quod.lib.umich.edu/l/lincoln/lincoln2/1:526.1?rgn=div2;view=fulltext

CPSIA information can be obtained at www.ICGtesting.com
Printed in the USA
LVOW05s0518051114

411991LV00033B/2680/P

9 780968 129111